BIG ENGLISH 3 PLUS

Mario Herrera • Christopher Sol Cruz

PUPIL'S BOOK

Contents

CLIL/Culture	Writing	Phonics		I can...
Science: Keeping clean bacteria, cough, decay, germs, gum disease, health, healthy, ill, skin, sneeze, sweat **Around the World: Time zones** chat, dark, different, e-pals, globe, half-turn, map, online, Time Zone	Sentence: Subjects and Verbs	**a_e, i_e, o_e** cake, face, game, shape bike, like, time, ride bone, home, note	Do your chores.	...talk about what people do before and after school. ...talk about different times of the day. ...talk about keeping clean. ...find and use adverbs of frequency, subjects and verbs.
Social Science: Creative jobs create, drawings, galleries, materials, paintings, photo shoot, piece of art, professional, sculptures, unusual **Around the World: Communities** be proud of, collect, community, contest, donate, get lost, rubbish	Sentence: Two Subjects and Verbs	**sm, st, sp, sk** smart, smile, smoke star, stop, storm space, Spain, spoon skates, ski, skin	Respect others.	...talk about what people do and where they work. ...talk about creative jobs. ...find and use two subjects and two verbs.
Maths: Pocket money adult, cash, cost, earn, let (someone) know, save, stranger, tidy, wash **Around the World: Chores** business, entrance, noodles, pavement, share, shovel, task, tiring	Paragraph: Titles	**ay, oy** day, May, pay, ray, say, way boy, joy, soy, toy	Always be happy to help.	...talk about how often people do things. ...talk about what people like/don't like doing and have to do. ...talk about chores and pocket money. ...use capital letters in titles.
Science: Camouflage blend in, bottom of the sea, desert, rainforest, stone, surroundings, tree bark **Around the World: Pets** alligators, canaries, geckos, goldfish, parakeets, rodents, snakes, tarantulas	Paragraph: Topic Sentences	**ea, oi, oe** bean, eat, meat, peach, sea, tea boil, coin, oil foe, toe	Protect animals and their habitats.	...talk about what animals can/can't do and where they're found. ...find and use adverbs. ...find and use topic sentences.
Geography: Climate average, climate, degrees Celsius, desert, dry, extreme, mild, minus **Around the World: Weather** cricket, fill up, kite, sledging, snow fight	Paragraph: Detail Sentences	**sc, sw, sn, sl** scar, scarf, scout swan, sweet, swim snack, snail, snow sleep, slim, slow	Prepare for the weather.	...talk about the weather today and in the past. ...talk about clothes. ...talk about climates around the world. ...find and use detail sentences.
Science: Animal senses avoid, brain, danger, echo, information, senses, sound waves, taste buds, tongue **Around the World: Jobs** clean, dreadful, fresh, look after, smelly, stink, wet	Paragraph: Final Sentences	**fl, pl, gl, bl** flag, flip-flops, fly plant, play, plum glad, glass, glow black, block, blow	Try new things.	...describe how things look, feel, taste, smell or sound. ...talk about the five senses in people and animals. ...find and use final sentences.
Science: Vitamins blood, bone, brain, energy, fat/water, healthy, iron, muscle, soluble, skin, teeth, vitamin **Around the World: Breakfasts** blueberries, boiled/fried eggs, cereal, doughnut, honey, oats, porridge, toast	Paragraphs	**br, cr, dr, fr, gr, pr, tr** bread, brick cream, cry dream, drive frog, from grass, green train, troll	Try different foods.	...ask and answer about food. ...talk about vitamins and how they help my body. ...find different parts of a paragraph.
P.E.: Keeping healthy active, activities, body, burn, calorie, fit, measure, put on weight, rest **Around the World: Strange sports** contest, court, diving, net, puck, race, regatta, rowing, scuba, team	Combining Sentences with *and, but, or*	**all, au, aw** all, ball, call, tall, wall haul, Paul claw, draw, law, yawn	Get exercise.	...talk about healthy and unhealthy habits. ...ask and answer about activities in the past. ...use *and, or* and *but* in sentences.
Art: Paintings artist, colourful, funny, happy, impressionist, oil painting, painter, sad, sketch, strange, watercolour **Around the World: Stage performances** dramatic, entertainment, flamenco, open-air theatre, performance, play, popular, puppet, show, stage	Writing Sentences	**nt, ld, nd, st** ant, plant, tent child, cold, old band, hand, sand chest, fast, nest	Recognise your talents.	...talk about actions in the past and places to visit. ...talk about paintings. ...write sentences with a subject, verb and object.

unit 1 Wake Up!

 1 Listen, look and say.

Monday 13th May

1 wake up

2 eat breakfast

3 get dressed

4 go to school

5 go home

6 go to the park

7 play football

8 do my homework

9 play video games

10 watch TV

 2 Listen, find and say.

 3 Play a game.

4 **Listen and sing. Does Kate eat breakfast?**

Hurry, Kate!

It's Monday, 7:30.
Kate has to wake up.
Her mum sees the clock and says
Wake up sleepy head.

Go, go, go! Hurry, Kate!
Hurry, Kate! You can't be late!

Kate eats breakfast, she gets dressed.
It's 7:45.
It's time to go to school.
And she can't be late!

Chorus

Kate's got her backpack
And she's got her lunch.
What time is it now?
Oh, no, it's time to go!

Chorus

5 **Read, match and say. Ask and answer.**

1	7:00	**a**	seven forty-five
2	7:30	**b**	seven fifty-five
3	7:45	**c**	seven o'clock
4	7:55	**d**	seven thirty
5	4:45	**e**	five twenty-five
6	4:00	**f**	four forty-five
7	8:15	**g**	four o'clock
8	5:25	**h**	eight fifteen

When does she wake up?

She wakes up at seven o'clock.

 **THINK BIG** **Which activities do you do inside? Which do you do outside?**

Story

 6 **7**

Listen and read. What does Luke do after school?

I Love Mondays!

Good morning, Mum! What day is it today?

It's Monday.

Hooray! I love Mondays!

1 Luke wakes up and goes into the kitchen.

Before lunch, at eleven ten, I've got Art. Art is fun!

But…

2 Before school, Luke always eats breakfast.

We draw pictures. We paint. It's great!

But today…

3 After breakfast, he brushes his teeth. Then he washes his face.

After lunch, at two fifteen, we've got English. I love English!

But Luke…

4 He gets dressed.

5 He puts on his shoes. He's ready for school.

6 But there's no school today!

7 **Read and say before school or after school.**

1 Luke eats breakfast.

2 Luke gets dressed.

3 Luke plays football.

4 Luke puts on his shoes.

5 Luke wakes up.

6 Luke plays basketball.

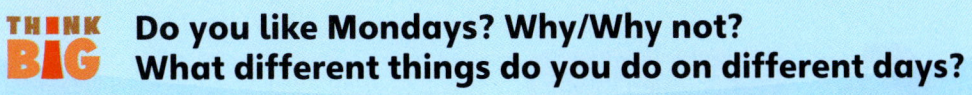

THINK BIG **Do you like Mondays? Why/Why not? What different things do you do on different days?**

8 🎧 **Listen and look at the sentences. Help Luke and Amy make more.**

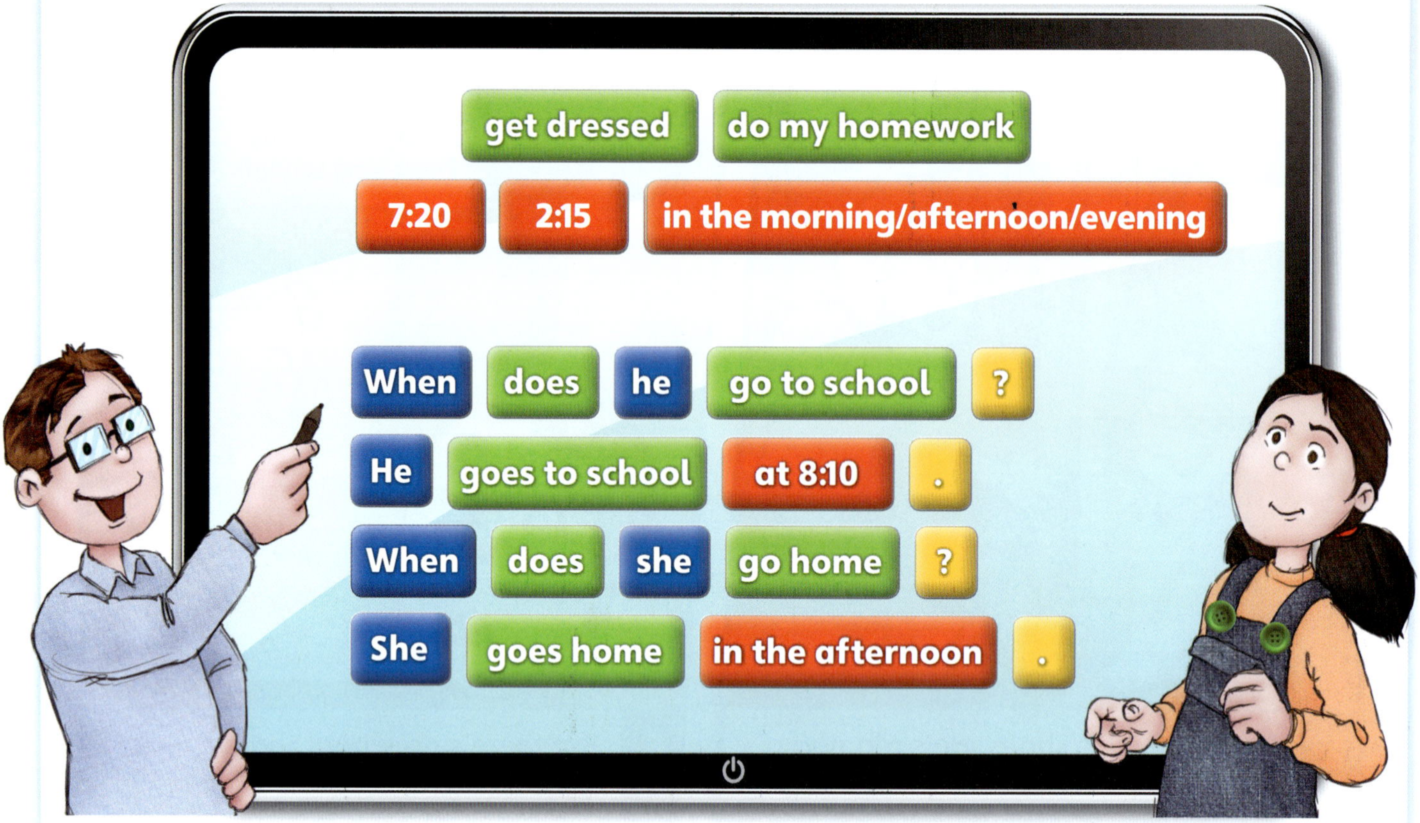

| get dressed | do my homework |

| 7:20 | 2:15 | in the morning/afternoon/evening |

When | does | he | go to school | ?

He | goes to school | at 8:10 | .

When | does | she | go home | ?

She | goes home | in the afternoon | .

9 **Read and match. Make sentences with a partner.**

1 Sam eats breakfast at 7:30
2 Jack wakes up at
3 Paula gets
4 Esteban does his homework in
5 Sandra plays video
6 Alice watches

a games at 5:00 in the afternoon.
b in the morning.
c TV at 8:00 in the evening.
d dressed at 7:50 in the morning.
e 6:45 in the morning.
f the afternoon.

10 **Look at 9. Ask and answer.**

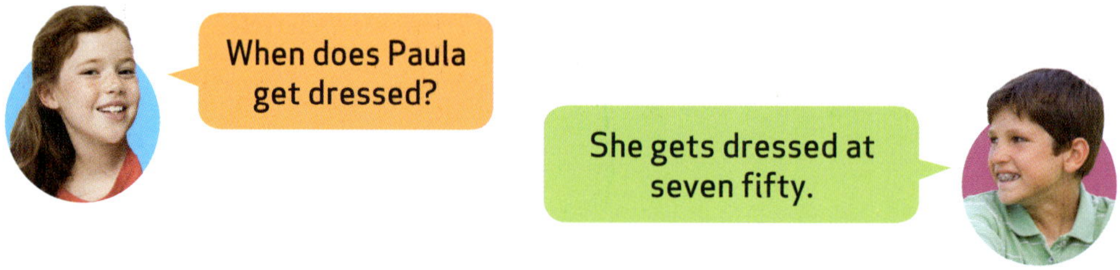

When does Paula get dressed?

She gets dressed at seven fifty.

11 Listen and find the clocks.

a

b

c

d

12 What does Claudia do before and after school? Make sentences.

Claudia's Schedule

6:30
wake up

3:20
go home

7:00
get dressed

6:45
get up

3:30
ride my bike

5:30
play football

4:45
do my homework

7:15
eat breakfast

6:30
eat dinner

7:30
go to school

13 Look at 12. What does Claudia do in the morning, afternoon and evening?

 Claudia wakes up at 6:30 in the morning.

She plays football in the afternoon.

 14 **Read and choose. Discuss with a partner.**

Why do we brush our teeth?

a to make them white

b to get rid of food

c to keep them strong

 15 **Listen and read. What are bacteria? Then check your answer in 14.**

Keep It Clean!

CONTENT WORDS
bacteria cough decay germs
gum disease health healthy
ill skin sneeze sweat

Question: Why is it important to shower, brush my teeth and wash my hands?
Max, 10

Having a Shower

People shower to look and feel good but also to keep clean and healthy. We can't always see it with our eyes but we get dirty all the time. We use warm water and soap to wash away sweat, dead skin and bacteria. Bacteria are tiny things that live on our skin. They can sometimes make us ill so make sure you wash your whole body well.

Brushing Your Teeth

We brush our teeth to keep them strong and healthy. It's good to do this after every meal but most people brush them twice a day: once in the morning after breakfast and once at night before going to bed. Brushing our teeth for about two minutes cleans away bacteria that can cause tooth decay and gum disease.

Washing Your Hands

Washing your hands is also very important. Every day our hands pick up millions of germs that can make us ill. Washing them with soap and water for at least 20 seconds gets rid of germs. Wash your hands before you eat, after you go to the toilet, after you cough or sneeze and any other time they get dirty.

 **THINK BIG** **What other things can you do to stay healthy? Where can we learn about staying healthy?**

16 **Look at 15. Read and say true or false.**

1 We shower to wash away bacteria from our body.

2 Sometimes we are dirty but we can't see it.

3 There are no bacteria in our mouth.

4 Brushing our teeth after every meal causes gum disease.

5 We pick up germs when we touch things with our hands.

6 Germs can't make you ill.

17 **What do you do every morning? Put the activities in order. Then compare with a partner.**

a Brush teeth

c Have a shower

e Get dressed

g Wash hands

b Brush hair

d Clean ears

f Have breakfast

h Go to the toilet

When do you brush your teeth?

I brush my teeth after breakfast and before I get dressed.

PROJECT

18 **Make a Keep it Clean poster. Then present it to the class.**

Eat healthy food.

Brush your teeth twice a day. It keeps them clean and healthy.

I eat healthy food and I brush my teeth twice a day.

Grammar

19 Look, listen and point. Then say.

a

> I often have fruit for breakfast. I sometimes have watermelon. I never have cereal for breakfast.

b

> I always eat cereal for breakfast. I usually drink juice, too. I never eat eggs for breakfast.

I **always** eat cereal. *****
I **usually** drink juice. ****
I **often** have fruit. ***
I **sometimes** eat bread. *
I **never** eat eggs.

He **always** eats breakfast.
Does he **always** eat breakfast?
He doesn't **always** eat breakfast.
BUT
He **sometimes** eats/doesn't eat eggs.
Sometimes he eats/doesn't eat eggs.
He eats/doesn't eat eggs **sometimes**.

20 Look at **19**. Complete the sentences.

How often do you

... drink milk with your breakfast?

1 I ❓ drink milk with my breakfast! Milk is good! *****
(Sam, 9)

2 I don't like milk very much. I ❓ eat yoghurt. ****
(Trish, 10)

... eat eggs for breakfast?

3 I ❓ eat eggs for breakfast. They're OK. *
(Nathan, 10)

4 I ❓ eat eggs for breakfast. I don't like eggs!
(Sonia, 10)

... eat fruit for breakfast?

5 I ❓ eat fruit but not every day. *
(Bea, 10)

6 I ❓ drink fresh orange juice. It's the same, isn't it? ***
(Jordan, 9)

21 **Look at the chart. Ask and answer.**

	*****	****	***	*	
Chloe	get up at 7 a.m.		watch TV after school		
Mario		take the bus to school			
Peter				play online games with his friends	go to bed after 10 p.m.
Eva	eat a salad for lunch				

1 Chloe/often/get up at 8 a.m.?

2 Mario/always/walk to school?

3 Peter/usually/play computer games on his own?

4 Eva/often/eat pasta for lunch?

5 Chloe/usually/do her homework after school?

6 Peter/sometimes/go to bed after 10 p.m.?

> Does Chloe often get up at 8 a.m.?

> No, she doesn't. She always gets up at 7a.m.

22 **Read and choose the correct answer.**

1 Do you watch TV?

a I don't usually watch TV.

b I often don't watch TV.

c I don't watch sometimes TV.

3 Do you like cola?

a Always I don't drink cola.

b I don't drink never cola.

c I don't often drink cola.

2 Do you always go to bed at 9 p.m.?

a Often I don't go to bed that early.

b I don't always go to bed that early.

c I don't go to bed that early always.

4 What do you do when you're ill?

a I don't go usually to school.

b Always I don't go to school.

c Sometimes I don't go to school.

23 **Look, read and write.**

On weekdays,[1] ❓ at 7 a.m. and get ready for school. [2] ❓ breakfast with my mum and my brother. [3] ❓ breakfast with us. He's a doctor and [4] ❓ for work very early. How about you? [5] ❓ breakfast with your family? What [6] ❓ for breakfast?

1	I	get up	always
2	I	have	usually
3	Dad	not have	always
4	he	leave	sometimes
5	you	have	always
6	you	have	usually

Time Zones

1 Look at your watch. What's the time now? Is it the same for everyone around the world? No, it isn't. That's because the world is divided into time zones. Look at the globe to find out why. When it's light in Hong Kong (A), it's still dark in New York (B). In fact, it isn't even the same day! This happens because the earth makes a half-turn in 12 hours so New York sees the new day 12 hours after Hong Kong. When it's 8:00 on Monday morning in Hong Kong, it's still 8:00 p.m. on Sunday evening in New York!

2 Sometimes there are different time zones in the same country. Look at the map of the United States. Because it's a very big country, it's got four different time zones.

24 **Look at the globe. Why is it daytime in some countries and nighttime in others?**

25 ¹⁴ **Listen and read. Where do the children live?**

> **CONTENT WORDS**
> chat   dark   different   e-pals   globe   half-turn   map   online   time zone

26 **Look at 25. Read and choose.**

1 When it's daytime in Hong Kong, it's **daytime/nighttime** in New York.

2 In Hong Kong, the day starts 12 hours **before/after** it starts in New York.

3 Hong Kong and New York are in the same **time zone/day** for only 12 hours.

4 There are different time zones in different parts of **all/some** countries.

5 For Marcus, the day changes **before/after** it changes for Maria.

6 Kara goes to bed **before/after** everyone else.

Maria

Marcus

³ These four e-pals live in different parts of the country. Let's say it's 10:30 a.m. for Kara in California. She's in class. She isn't hungry yet because she always has a good breakfast. In Montana, it's 11:30 a.m. and John is already thinking about lunch. He's hungry and he can't wait for the long break! For Maria, in Texas, it's 12:30 p.m. She and her friends are eating sandwiches for lunch. It's 1:30 p.m. in Washington, DC, and Marcus is putting his empty lunchbox into his bag. He's getting ready for his afternoon class.

⁴ The four friends have the same bedtime. They often chat online in the evenings but they need to make sure that the time is right for everyone!

John

Kara

27 **Talk with a partner. These people live in different time zones. What do you think they're doing right now?**

1 Emma – Anchorage, Alaska: Sunday 10:15 a.m.
2 Carlos – Mexico City, Mexico: Sunday 13:15 p.m.
3 Sophia – Greece, Athens: Sunday 9:15 p.m.
4 Jin – Beijing, China: Monday 2:15 a.m.

a having dinner at a restaurant
b having lunch at home
c having breakfast with all the family
d sleeping

I think Emma's having breakfast with her family. It's Sunday and they're all at home.

Or she's sleeping. I never get up before 11 a.m. on a Sunday!

THINK BIG It's ten o'clock in the morning where you are. Find out what time it is in Buenos Aires, Cairo and Sydney.

28 **Read and find.**

> A sentence has got a subject and a verb.
> She eats breakfast before school.

1 I ride my bike to school.

29 **Find the subjects and verbs. Compare with your partner.**

1 Andrew eats lunch at 12:30.

2 Marcia goes to school at 8:05.

3 We go home at 3:50 in the afternoon.

4 My brother does his homework at 4:30.

5 You eat dinner with your family in the evening.

30 **What's missing, subject or verb? Make new sentences and compare with a partner.**

1 Bridget ❓ at 6:45 in the morning.

2 ❓ eats breakfast at 7:00.

3 Her ❓ goes to the park with friends.

4 Beth ❓ after school with her family.

5 ❓ get dressed in the morning.

31 **Read about Jack's day. Change all the information in blue and red. Write a new paragraph.**

Jack wakes up at six ten in the morning. He has a shower and gets dressed before school. He rides a bike to school and gets there at eight o'clock. His brother gets to school at eight ten. Jack plays football after school in the park. He does his homework at five fifteen. The family eat dinner together and then they watch TV.

32 **Write four sentences about your day. Read them to your partner.**

 **33** **Listen, read and repeat.**

1 a_e   **2** i_e   **3** o_e

 34 **Listen and find. Then say.**

face   **bike**   **bone**

 35 **Listen and blend the sounds.**

1 g-a-me   game   **2** c-a-ke   cake
3 t-i-me   time   **4** n-o-te   note
5 h-o-me   home   **6** sh-a-pe   shape
7 r-i-de   ride   **8** l-i-ke   like

 36 **Read aloud. Then listen and chant.**

What time is it?
It's time to play a game.
What time is it?
It's time to eat cake.
What time is it?
It's time to ride a bike.
What time is it?
It's time to go home.

37 **Look, listen and point.**

21

a

I feed the dog
before school.

b

I clean my room
after school.

c

I wash the dishes
after dinner.

PROJECT

38 **What chores do you do at home? Copy the chart in your notebook and ✓. Then ask three classmates about their chores.**

CHORES

Chore	Me	1	2	3
feed pet				
clean my room				
wash the dishes				

39 **Read and choose.**

¹When/What does Mia wake up on Friday? She **²wakes/wake** up at seven fifteen because she has a shower, gets dressed, eats breakfast and brushes her teeth **³before/after** school. She goes to school **⁴at/in** eight o'clock. School finishes at three thirty in the **⁵morning/afternoon**. When **⁶do/does** she do her homework? At four fifteen. Then she goes **⁷to/at** the park and **⁸plays/playing** baseball with her friends.

40 **Make five sentences in your notebook about things you do or don't do before and after school. Use always, usually, often, sometimes or never.**

41 **Play the Silly Sentences game.**

6:15 in the evening

eat breakfast

Jack eats breakfast at six fifteen in the evening.

That's silly!

I Can

- talk about what people do before and after school.
- talk about different times of the day.
- talk about keeping clean.
- find and use adverbs of frequency, subjects and verbs.

unit 2
Lots of Jobs!

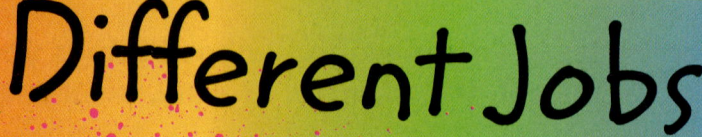

22

1 Listen, look and say.

Different Jobs

1 firefighter

2 police officer

3 cashier

4 waiter

5 farmer

6 scientist

7 nurse

8 student

23

2 Listen, find and say.

3 Play a game.

4 Listen and sing. How many jobs are in the song?

Working Together

There are many people
In our community.
So many jobs to do,
So many places to be.

Working together, working hard.
Nurse, farmer, teacher and chef.

Where does she work?
What does she do?
She's a nurse
And she always helps you.

Chorus

Where does he work?
What does he do?
He's a firefighter
And he's very brave, too.

5 Match the jobs in 1 to the places. Make sentences.

a
at a hospital

b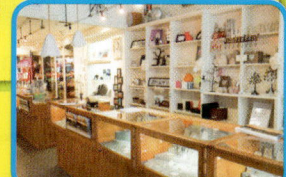
at a shop

c
at a fire station

d
at a university

e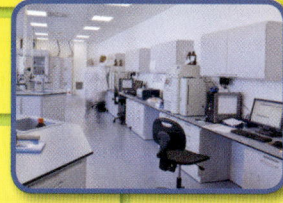
at a laboratory

f
at a police station

g
at a restaurant

h
on a farm

 A student studies at a university.

A scientist works at a laboratory.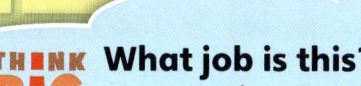

THINK BIG **What job is this?**
"I sometimes work at night. I sometimes work in the day.
I wear a uniform. I often work with another person."

27

 6 Listen and read. What does Luke's mum do?

1 Luke and his dad are at the hospital.

2 They want to find Luke's mum.

3 Luke's mum is at work.

4 Luke's mum works at the hospital.

5 Luke's mum isn't a doctor or a nurse.

6 Luke's mum is a cashier. She works at a shop. It's her birthday today!

7 **Read and complete the sentences. Then say.**

1 Luke is looking for his ❓ .
2 Luke's mum works at the ❓ .
3 Luke's mum isn't a doctor or a ❓ .
4 Luke's mum is a ❓ .
5 Today it's Luke's mum's ❓ .

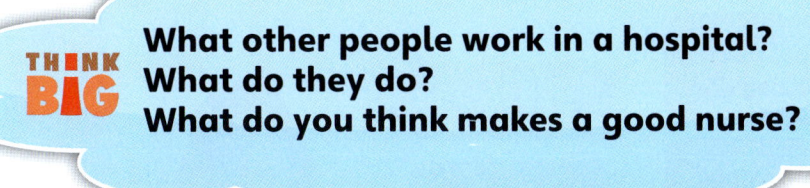

THINK BIG
What other people work in a hospital?
What do they do?
What do you think makes a good nurse?

Language in Action

28

8 **Listen and look at the sentences. Help Luke and Amy make more.**

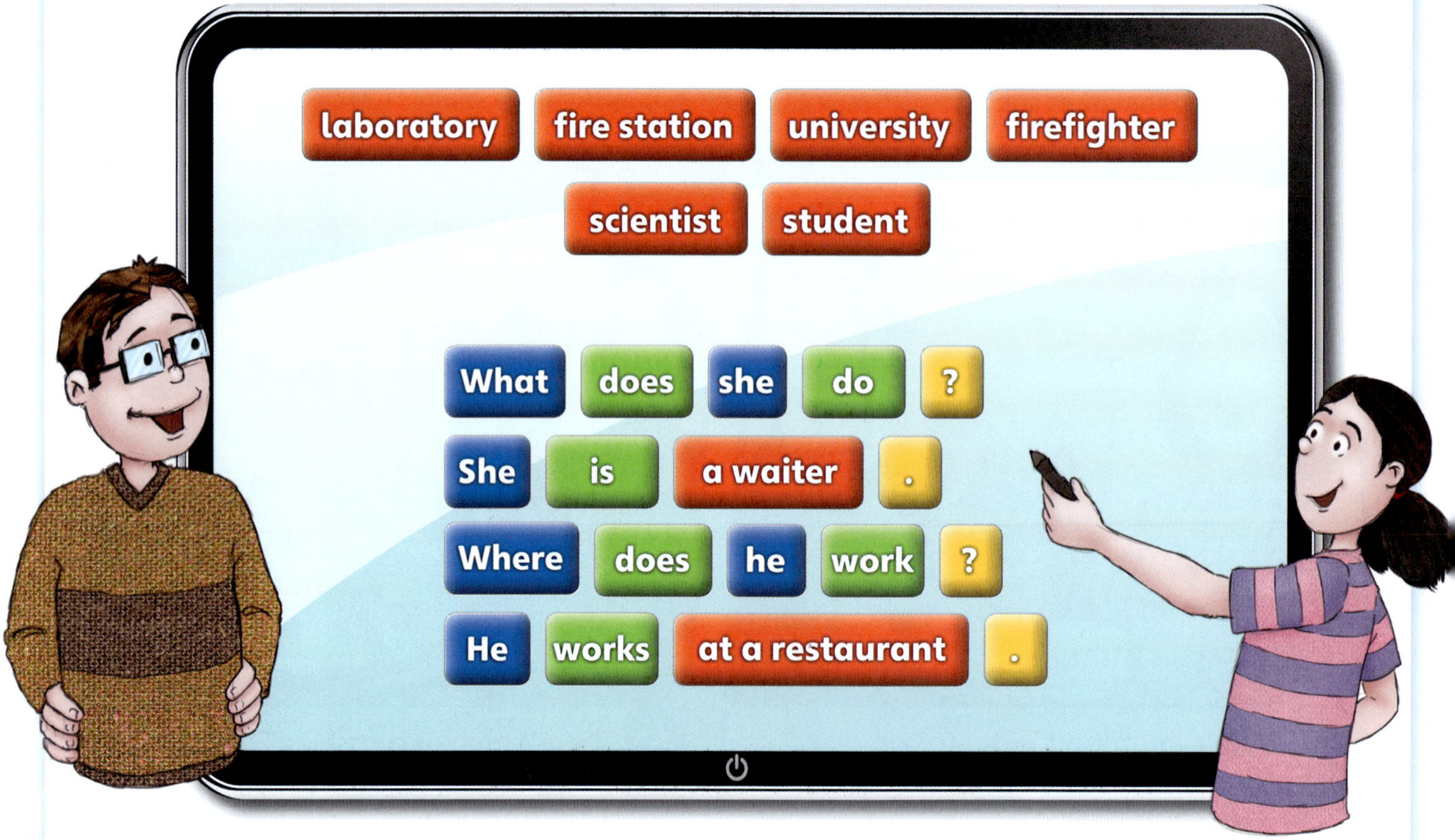

laboratory   fire station   university   firefighter

scientist   student

What does she do ?

She is a waiter .

Where does he work ?

He works at a restaurant .

9 **Put the dialogue in order with a partner. Then change the words in red and make new dialogues.**

a **She** works **at a school**.

b What does your **mum** do?

c **She's** a **nurse**.

d Where does **she** work?

10 **What about you? Ask and answer about your family.**

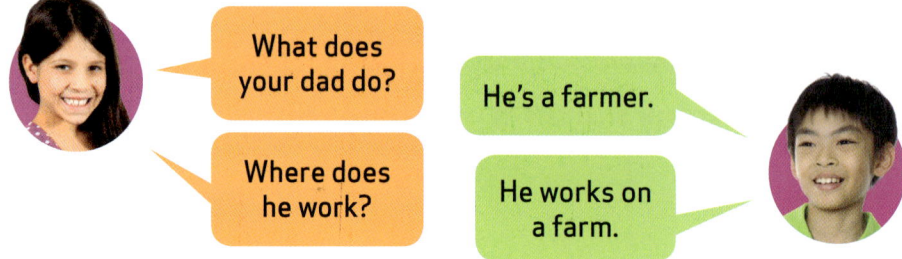

What does your dad do?

He's a farmer.

Where does he work?

He works on a farm.

30

11 **Listen and match.**

1 Megan

a

c

b

2 Susan

3 Ellie

12 **Read and choose.**

1 **What/Why** does your grandad do? He's a cashier and he works in a shop.
2 **When/Where** do Paul and Leyla study? They study at university.
3 Where **do/does** Alice work? She works at a fire station.
4 What do you **do/does**? I'm a doctor.
5 I work **on/in** a farm. I'm a farmer.
6 We work **at/on** a hospital.

13 **Look and make questions and answers.**

1 **a** what/brothers/do?
   scientists
  b where/work?
   laboratory
2 **a** what/you/do?
   teacher
  b where/work?
   school
3 **a** what/mum/do?
   firefighter
  b where/she/work?
   fire station

What do your
brothers do?

They're scientists.

Discuss with a partner.

What do you enjoy doing?

I like drawing. It makes me feel happy.

 Listen and read. Which of these people sell their work to magazines?

The Work Files:
Creative Jobs

CONTENT WORDS
create   drawings   galleries
materials   paintings   photo shoot
piece of art   professional
sculptures   unusual

People spend a big part of their lives at work so it's very important to choose the right job. When you do something you really enjoy, you feel happy. Today we're having a look at creative jobs. Would you like to do one of them?

Artist

Professional artists usually go to art school. They learn to use different materials to create a work of art. They use pencils to make drawings, oil paints, acrylics or water colours to make paintings, metal or wood to make other works of art. Some artists like to work with unusual materials like chewing gum, buttons or plastic supermarket bags! Artists show their work in art galleries. A work of art can be very expensive.

Photographer

Photographers travel a lot and take photos of people and places all over the world. Their work is sometimes difficult or dangerous, like when they take photos of wild animals. Serious photographers never go out without their camera. They don't want to miss a good photo. They sell their photos to websites, newspapers, magazines and television news programmes. They also sell books with their photos.

Fashion Designer

Fashion designers create the clothes we wear. First, they draw sketches with their ideas. Then they cut patterns to make dresses, trousers, coats and many more things. Designing clothes can be great fun. Fashion designers show their work in fashion shows or do photo shoots for magazines. They sell their clothes in shops or online.

 **THINK BIG** **What other creative jobs can you think of?**
What talents do you need to do a creative job?

16 Look at **15**. Read and complete. Use the words from the box.

> camera   happy   pattern   sketch   unusual   world

1 When you like your job you feel ❓ .
2 Chewing gum is a(n) ❓ material to use for a work of art.
3 Photographers often travel all over the ❓ for their work.
4 Photographers like to have their ❓ with them all the time.
5 When they have a good idea, fashion designers draw a ❓ .
6 Clothes are cut using a ❓ .

17 Interview a partner. Take notes in your notebook. Share with the class.

1 Do you like art? Have you got a favourite work of art?
2 What kind of photos do you like to look at (wild animals, fashion, etc)?
3 Do you like fashion? What kind of clothes do you usually wear?

PROJECT

18 Make a **Creative Job** presentation. Then present it to the class.

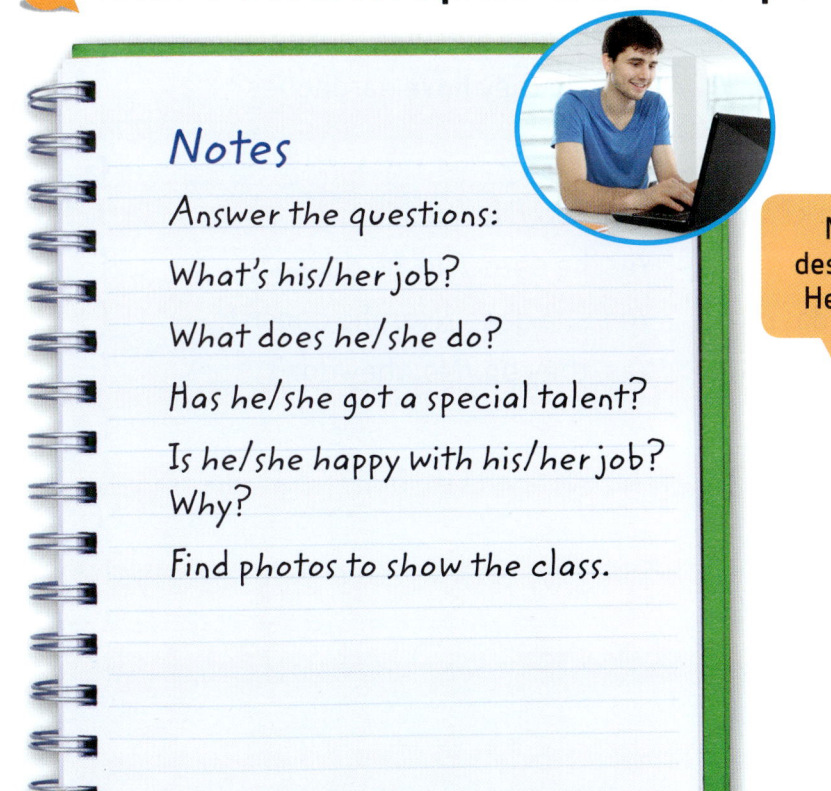

Notes
Answer the questions:
What's his/her job?
What does he/she do?
Has he/she got a special talent?
Is he/she happy with his/her job? Why?
Find photos to show the class.

Mark Willows is a video game designer. He creates video games. He knows a lot about computers.

He's very happy with his job because it's fun!

34

19 **Listen and read. What's the man's job?**

At the Oscars…

Reporter: Can you answer some questions, please?

Man: Who, me? OK.

Reporter: Where do you live?

Man: I live in Park Street.

Reporter: What sports do you play?

Man: I play basketball. Er… Excuse me. Do I know you?

Reporter: No, but I know you. You're one of the actors.

Man: No, I'm not.

Reporter: But you're wearing a black suit!

Man: I always wear a black suit to work! I'm a waiter!

I **wear** a black suit to work.	**What do** you **wear** to work?
He **lives** in Park Street.	**Where does** he **live**?
She **plays** music every day.	**When does** she **play** music?
They **like** listening to music.	**Why do** they **have** earphones?

Do I **wear** a black suit to work?	Yes, I do./No, I don't.
Does he **live** in Park Street?	Yes, he does./No, he doesn't.
Does she **play** music every day?	Yes, she does./No, she doesn't.
Do they **like** listening to music?	Yes, they do./No, they don't.

I **don't wear** a black suit to work.
He **doesn't live** in Park Street.
She **doesn't play** music every day.
They **don't like** listening to music.

20 Read and complete.

1 Dan ❓ cartoons on TV on Saturday morning.   (watch)
2 ❓ they ❓ their car on the weekend?   (wash)
3 Jack ❓ his black bag everywhere.   (carry)
4 My parents ❓ in an office.   (not work)
5 ❓ Patrick ❓ in Vine Street?   (live)
6 Maria ❓ her hair every day.   (not brush)

21 Correct the sentences using the words in brackets.

1 Mehmet works in a hospital. (office)
   Mehmet ❓ in a hospital. He ❓
2 The twins play football. (basketball)
   The twins ❓
3 He sees his grandad every weekend. (every month)
   He ❓
4 You live in New York. (Seattle)
   I ❓
5 He knows a famous actor. (famous TV chef)
   He ❓
6 The players wear red T-shirts. (blue T-shirts)
   The players ❓

22 Complete the questions and answers.

1 Brad/star ✓
   Does Brad ❓ in a new film?
   Yes, he ❓.
2 they/ask ✗
   ❓ you questions?
   ❓
3 you/cook ✓
   ❓ ?
   ❓
4 Ann/wear ✗
   ❓ a uniform to work?
   ❓
5 they/go ✓
   ❓ to school?
   ❓
6 your friend/watch ✗
   ❓ sports on TV?
   ❓

Making Communities Better

1   People often say "We want to make the world a better place. But how? Where do we begin?" The answer is easy. Start with where you live. When we make our community a better place, we make the world better, too.

These children know this and they're happy to do something about it. Let's meet them and see what they do. Maybe we can get some ideas to help our communities, too.

2   Lalana lives in Chiang Mai, Thailand. She knows that many schools in her city haven't got money to buy books. Lalana and her friends ask people to donate books. They collect the books and take them to schools in their city. Many schools have now got more and better books, thanks to Lalana and her friends.

Lalana

23 Discuss in groups.

Do you live in a big or a small community? What's it like?

What do you like about the place?

What do you like about the people?

35

24 Listen and read. Who helps tourists in their city?

> **CONTENT WORDS**
> be proud of collect community contest
> donate get lost rubbish

25 Look at 24. Correct the mistakes. Write new sentences.

1   We don't change the world when we do things for our community. ❓

2   In Chiang Mai, schools donate books to people. ❓

3   Barcelona doesn't have many tourists. ❓

4   Tourists say bad things about Carla's city when they go back home. ❓

5   Marcus rides his bike to school. ❓

6   Marcus and his friends pick up the rubbish but they don't enjoy it. ❓

3   Marcus lives in a small town near Melbourne, Australia. Every morning he walks to school. He sees a lot of rubbish along the road. He and his friends have a contest. They pick up the rubbish and they see who can collect the most. They clean up the streets and they have fun, too.

4   Carla lives in Barcelona, Spain. A lot of tourists visit her city every year and they often get lost. Carla likes helping people and she's proud of her city. At the weekends, she and her big sister help tourists find the places they're looking for. When the tourists go back home, they tell their friends that Barcelona is a wonderful place!

Marcus

Carla

5   See? It isn't difficult. When every one of us does one little thing for our community, we make it a great place to live.

26 **Talk with a partner. What can you do to help? Choose from a–d. Have you got any other ideas?**

1 Some old people live alone. They haven't got family and they can't go out.

2 Some younger children in your school aren't very good pupils.

3 Some people haven't got a job or a home. They live in the streets and they haven't got any money.

4 Your town is beautiful but it doesn't have many visitors because people don't know about it.

a Ask supermarkets to donate the food they can't sell.

b Make a webpage with photos and information about your town.

c Do their shopping for them.

d Help them with their lessons.

27 **Write in your notebook three ways you can help your community.**

THINK BIG Present your ideas in **27** to the class. Then vote to decide on the best three ways you can help your community.

28 **Read and find.**

> A sentence can have two subjects and two verbs.
> Al is a farmer. Matt is a farmer.
> Al and Matt are farmers.
> I live in Rome. I work in Rome.
> I live and work in Rome.

1 Julie and John are students. They live and study at a university.

29 **Write the sentences. Use and to make two subjects or two verbs.**

1 I live in a town. I work in a town.

2 Asya is a scientist. Alfonzo is a scientist.

3 My mother is a firefighter. My father is a firefighter.

4 I work at a restaurant. I eat at a restaurant.

5 My cousin lives in London. My cousin studies in London.

6 My sister lives on a farm. My brother lives on a farm.

30 **Complete the sentences for you. Then say.**

1 Before school, I ❓ .   **2** After school, I ❓ .

Before school, I eat breakfast and get dressed.

After school, I play football and do my homework.

31 Listen, read and repeat.

1 **sm**   2 **st**   3 **sp**   4 **sk**

 32 Listen and find. Then say.

smile   **st**op   **sp**oon   **sk**ates

 33 Listen and blend the sounds.

1	s-m-ar-t	smart	**2**	s-k-i-n	skin
3	S-p-ai-n	Spain	**4**	s-m-o-ke	smoke
5	s-k-i	ski	**6**	s-t-or-m	storm
7	s-t-ar	star	**8**	s-p-a-ce	space

34 Read aloud. Then listen and chant.

Stop and look.
Look at the stars,
The stars in space,
And smile!

Values | Respect others.

35 Look, listen and point.

a

Can I help you?

b

Please take my seat.

c

He's first.

SALE

2/€5

Only 99¢

BOB

PROJECT

36 Make a class book about respecting others.

37 **Listen and say yes or no.**

1 Julie's mum works at a hospital.

2 Her mum is a doctor.

3 Her dad is a student.

4 Her sisters work on a farm.

38 **Make questions. Then say.**

1 I'm a firefighter.

2 My brother works at a laboratory.

3 My dad is a police officer.

4 My two sisters are students.

5 My grandma works at a shop.

6 My uncles work at a hospital.

39 **Play the Jobs game.**

at a	fire station
	hospital
	laboratory
	police station
	restaurant
	shop
	university
on a	farm

I Can

- talk about what people do and where they work.

- talk about creative jobs.

- find and use two subjects and two verbs.

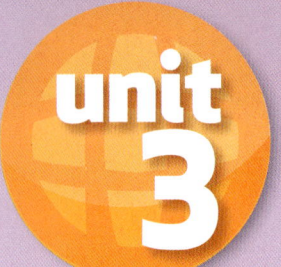

unit 3

Working Hard!

44

1 Listen, look and say.

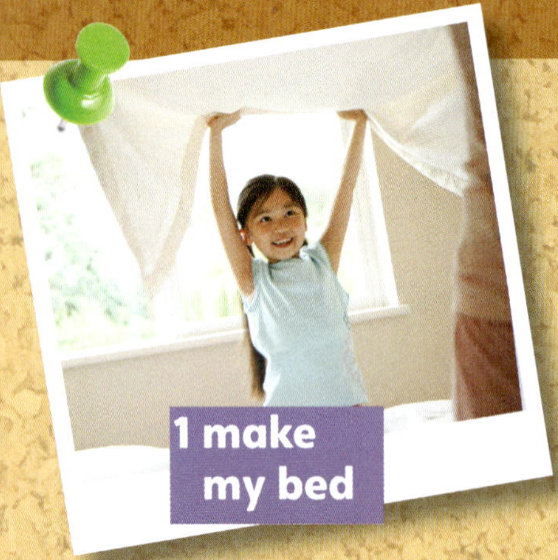

1 make my bed

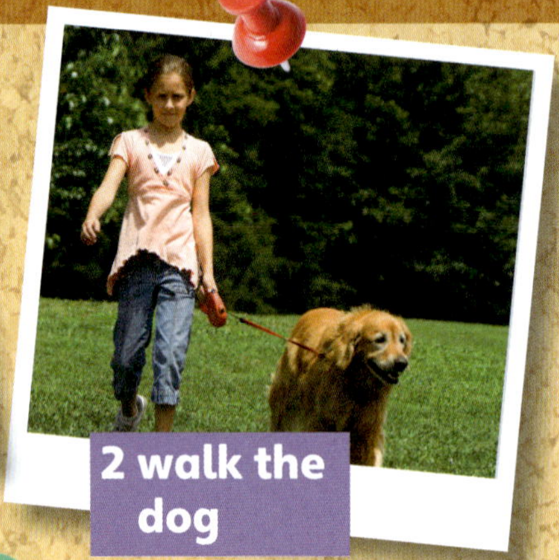

2 walk the dog

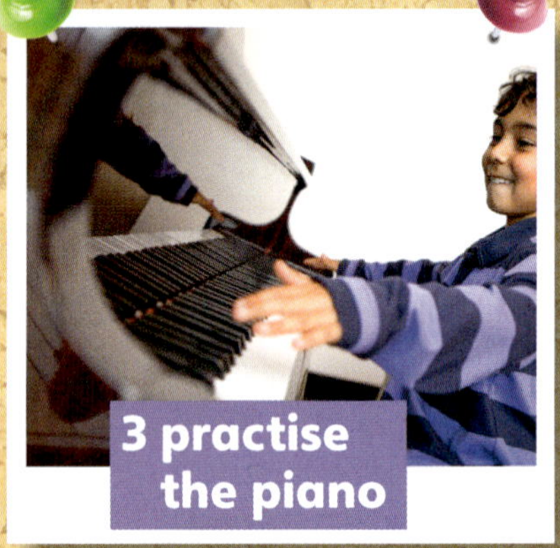

3 practise the piano

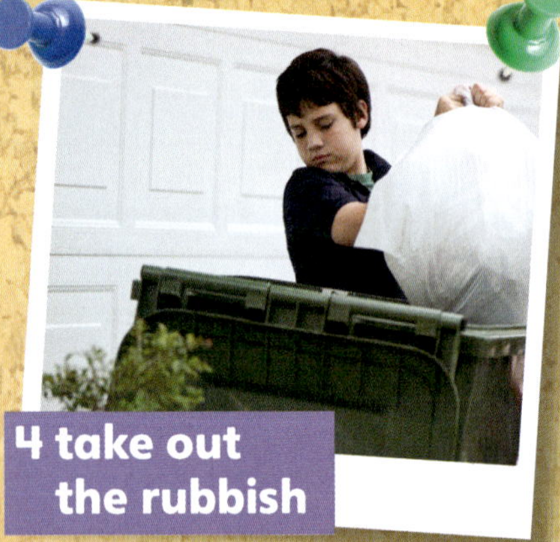

4 take out the rubbish

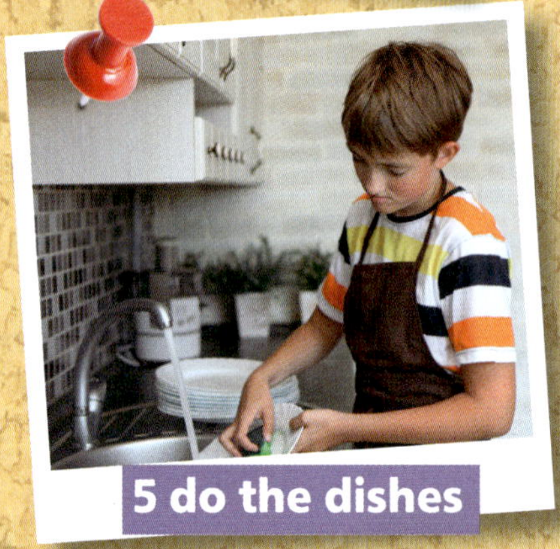

5 do the dishes

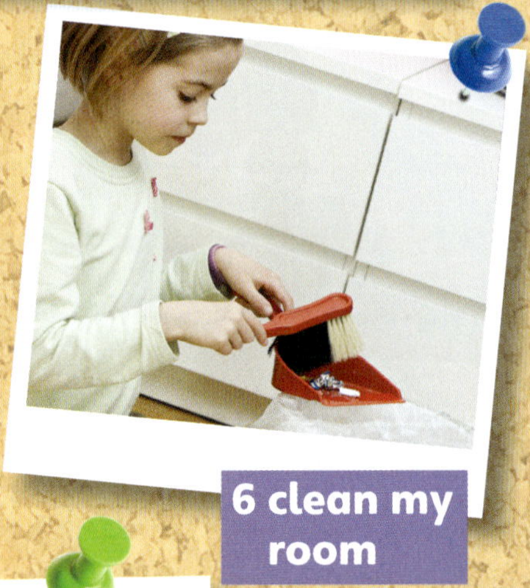

6 clean my room

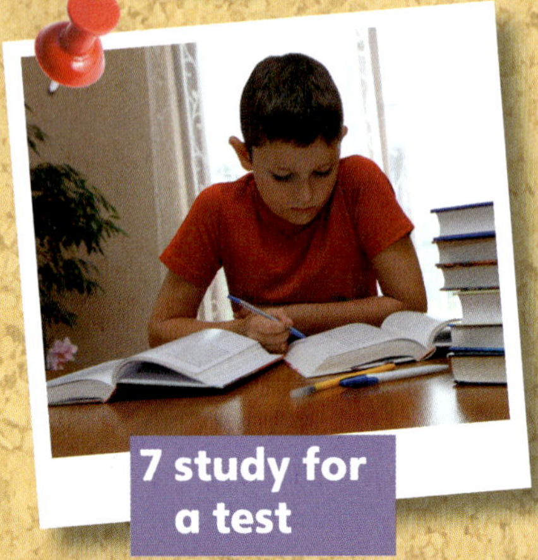

7 study for a test

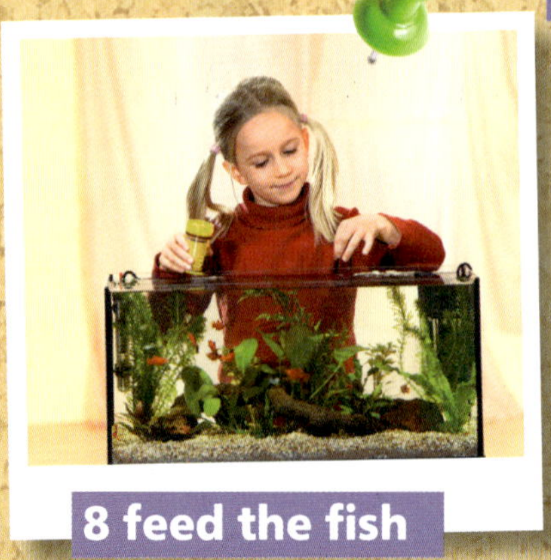

8 feed the fish

45

2 Listen, find and say.

3 Play a game.

4 Listen and sing. What chores does Matt do?

Different Twins

My name's Matt
And my name's Mike.
We want to talk to you.
I do my chores
And I do, too.
But we are not alike.

**Mike and Matt, Matt and Mike.
These two twins are not alike.**

I'm Matt, I always clean my room.
I do my chores each day.
I sometimes do the dishes
And then we go and play.

Chorus

I'm Mike, I always make my bed.
I do my chores each day.
I sometimes walk the dog
And then we go and play.

Chorus

5 Use the chart to ask and answer questions about Matt.

Matt	Mon	Tue	Wed	Thu	Fri	Sat	Sun
clean his room	✓	✓	✓	✓	✓	✓	✓
feed the fish	✓		✓		✓	✓	✓
do the dishes				✓			✓
take out the rubbish							

Does Matt clean his room?  Yes, he does.

THINK BIG Which of these are your favourite chores?
Why are chores important?

50

6 Listen and read. What time does Amy have to leave for school?

1 Amy is thinking. Her mum comes into her bedroom.

2 Amy likes making lists. She often makes a list of things she has to do.

3 Amy has to do lots of things before school.

4 Amy's clock still says 7:05.

5 What time does Amy have to leave? At 7:50? Oh, dear!

6 Amy's never late for school. She doesn't want to be late today!

7 **Read and say true or false.**

1 Amy has to do lots of things before school.

2 She has to eat breakfast.

3 She has to walk the dog.

4 She has to study for her English test.

5 She has to leave for school at 7:00.

6 She has to get a new alarm clock.

THINK BIG **What kinds of lists do people make?**
How do lists help us to remember things?
What other things help us to remember?

51
8 Listen and look at the sentences. Help Luke and Amy make more.

study for a test   do the dishes   make my bed

take out the rubbish

| What | do we | have to do | ? |

| We | have to | practise the piano | . |

| What | does she | have to do | ? |

| She | has to | walk the dog | . |

9 Follow the lines. What do they have to do?

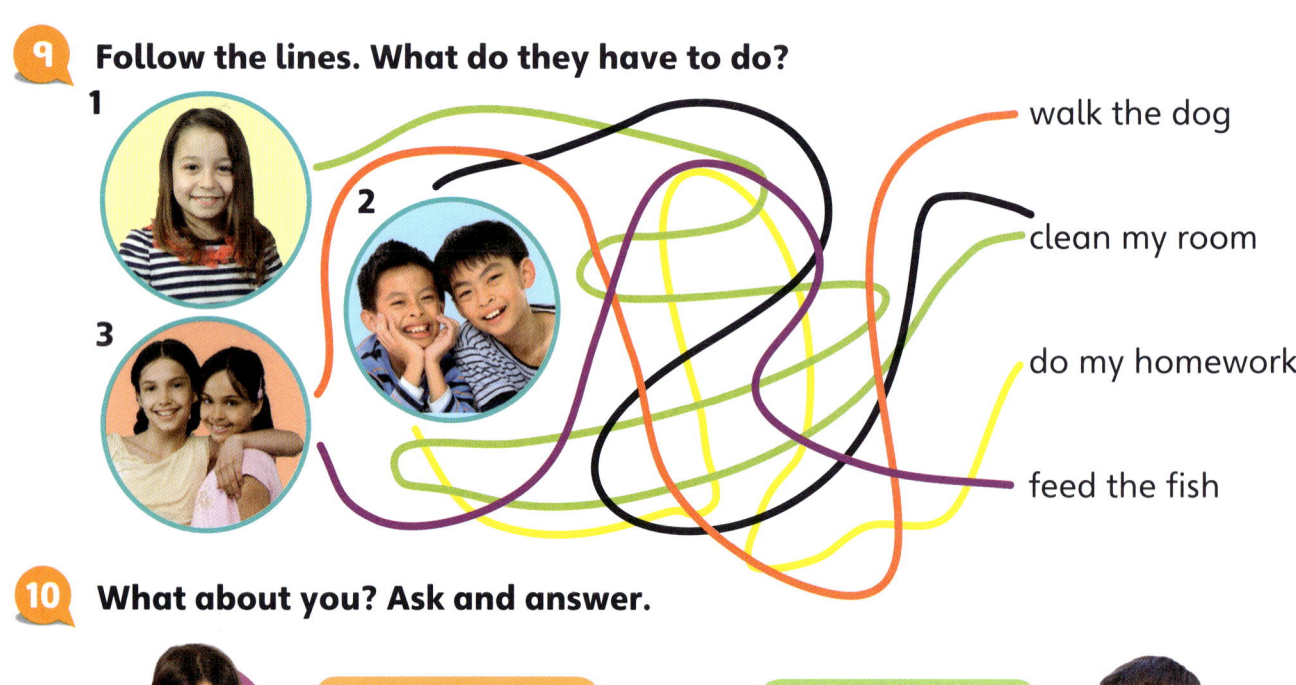

1

2

3

walk the dog

clean my room

do my homework

feed the fish

10 What about you? Ask and answer.

What do you have to do?

I have to practise the piano.

53

11 Listen to Alexia's week and find the three mistakes.

Monday	Tuesday	Wednesday	Thursday	Friday
do the dishes, practise the guitar	study for a test	take out the rubbish	make my bed	clean my room

12 Put the words in order. Then say.

1 sometimes | Do | make | your | bed? | you

2 do? | What | do | have | to | you

3 have | What | to | do? | Sally | does

4 never | the | dishes. | does | Jake

5 fish. | My | usually | feed | the | sisters

13 Look at the chart. Make sentences about Leo. Use **always**, **usually**, **sometimes** and **never**.

always ***	usually **	sometimes *	never X

Leo's chores	Mon	Tue	Wed	Thu	Fri
study for a test	✓		✓		
clean his room	✓	✓	✓		✓
make his bed	✓	✓	✓	✓	✓
do the dishes					

Do you get pocket money? What do you do when you want something expensive? Share with the class.

 Listen and read. Who can you work for?

54

CONTENT WORDS

adult   cash   cost   earn   let (someone) know
save   stranger   tidy   wash

Pocket Money

When you're a child, your parents take care of all your needs. You sometimes get a little pocket money to spend as you like, too. But when you want to buy something expensive, you need extra money. Where do you find it? You can't get a real job yet but there are ways you can earn some extra cash.

Help with the housework Everyone has to help around the house. You probably have to tidy your room and take out the rubbish. Do extra work to earn extra money. Ask your parents what extra things you can do for them and how much they can pay you for doing them.

Do chores for other people Sometimes other adult members of your family, friends or neighbours are very busy and they haven't got time to do some chores. Let them know how you can help. Write what you can do and how much it costs on a piece of paper, make copies and give them to the people you know.
Remember to be safe. Don't work for strangers. Always ask your parents and let them know where you are.

Save your money Save a little bit of the money you make each time. This way you always have extra cash!

To give you an idea of how much you can earn per week, look at Anne's chart:

	Amount	Number of times a week (x)	Subtotal
do the dishes	€1	3	€ ❓
make breakfast	€2	2	€ ❓
walk Mrs Porter's dog	50 cents	6	€ ❓
water Grandma's plants	€1	2	€ ❓
wash Uncle Joe's car	€5	1	€ ❓
			TOTAL: €

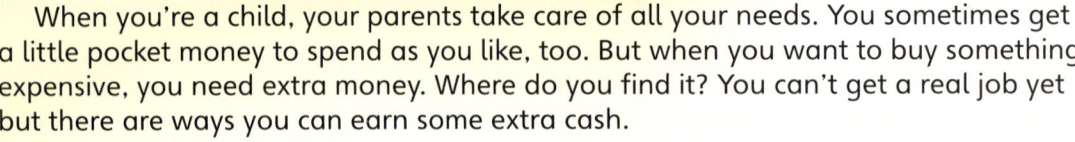

16 **Look at 15. Read and say true or false.**

1 Children can get a job to earn extra cash.

2 Everyone in the family has to do housework.

3 Parents pay their children for all the housework they do.

4 Some adults don't do their chores because they're busy.

5 Anne only works for family members.

17 **Do the sums and complete Anne's chart in 15. Then ask and answer.**

How much does Anne make from doing the dishes?

1 times 3 equals 3. She earns three euros a week from doing the dishes.

THINK BIG Is it better to spend or save pocket money? Why? How much of your pocket money should you save?

PROJECT

18 **Make a Chores chart to save money. Then present it to the class.**

You want to buy a tablet. It costs €400.
First, make a chart with chores you can do and how often you can do them.
Calculate how much money you can make per week.
Calculate how many weeks until you have €400.

I earn 1 euro each time I make my bed. I make my bed every day. 1 times 7 equals 7. I get 7 euros a week. 10 times 7 equals 70. So for 10 weeks, I get 70 euros!

My pocket money			
	Amount	Number of times	Subtotal
Make my bed	€1	7 times a week	€7 a week (€70 for 10 weeks)
Take out the rubbish			
Feed the cat			

19 Look, listen and point. Then say.

a

I hate tidying up! I like studying in an untidy bedroom. I hate studying in a tidy bedroom!

b

I love tidying up! I like studying in a tidy bedroom. I hate studying in an untidy bedroom!

I/We **like/love/hate** tidy**ing** up.
You **like/love/hate** gett**ing** up early.
He/She/It **likes/loves/hates** sleep**ing**.
They **like/love/hate** watch**ing** TV.

I/We **don't like/love/hate** tidy**ing** up.
You **don't like/love/hate** gett**ing** up early.
He/She/It **doesn't like/love/hate** sleep**ing**.
They **don't like/love/hate** watch**ing** TV.

Do I/we **like/love/hate** tidy**ing** up?
Do you **like/love/hate** gett**ing** up early?
Does he/she/it **like/love/hate** sleep**ing**?
Do they **like/love/hate** watch**ing** TV?

–ing

cook - cook**ing**
tidy - tidy**ing**
write - writ**ing**
shop - shop**ping**

20 Write the verbs in your notebook using **–ing**.

1 make ❓

2 do ❓

3 swim ❓

4 feed ❓

5 study ❓

6 sit ❓

21 **Read and complete. Use the correct form of the words from the box.**

cook   do   eat   get up   listen   swim

1 I don't like ❓ sweets. They're bad for your teeth.

2 Why does Jerry hate ❓ sports?

3 We like ❓ . It's relaxing!

4 She loves ❓ to loud music.

5 Do you like ❓ in the sea?

6 He doesn't like ❓ early in the morning.

22 **Do the quiz. Are you a home person?**

🟡 **love**   🔴 **like**   🟢 **don't like**   🔵 **hate**

1 I ❓ cleaning my room.

2 I ❓ tidying up the house.

3 I ❓ spending time at home.

4 I ❓ cooking with friends.

5 I ❓ washing dishes.

6 I ❓ having parties at my house.

Now find your score: love= 4 points   like= 3 points   don't like= 2 points   hate= 1 point

24–19   You love your home and you're a great host! Your friends are lucky!
18–12   You like being at home but you often have other things to do.
11–7   You let other people do all the work for you. Not nice!
6–1   Please don't invite me to your home!

23 **Ask and answer. Use like, love and hate. Write your partner's answers in your notebook.**

1 watch horror films?   ❓

2 play sports?   ❓

3 listen to classical music?   ❓

4 read comics?   ❓

5 eat fast food?   ❓

6 text?   ❓

Do you like watching horror films?

Yes, I do. I love watching horror films.

No, I don't like watching horror films. I like watching comedies.

24 **Use the information in 23 and write about your partner. Then share with the class.**

❓ likes/doesn't like ❓

Many Hands Make Light Work

1   Everyone knows that even difficult tasks can be easy to do if you have help. All around the world, families share not only the housework but also the chores of the family business. Parents do most of them but children help out when they can, too. Let's find out what chores these kids do.

2   Leah lives in Alaska. There's usually a lot of snow on the roads and the pavements. Everyone has to shovel snow to keep the entrance to their home clear. Leah shovels snow before she goes to school every day. Leah says, "I like shovelling snow!"

25 **Discuss with a partner. Then check with your teacher.**

What do you think the expression "Many hands make light work" means?

   a It means that when people work together, nothing goes right.

   b It means that when people work together, the work is easy.

Do you have an expression that means the same in your language?

57

26 **Listen and read. Then match.**

CONTENT WORDS

business   entrance   noodles
pavement   share   shovel
task   tiring

1 Leah   **a** in France.
2 Ivan   lives   **b** in Singapore.
3 Chen Wei   **c** in Alaska.

27 **Look at 26. Answer the questions.**

   1 What does Leah do to help at home?
   2 When does Leah do her chore?
   3 What does Chin Wei's mother do?
   4 Why does Chin Wei help his mother?
   5 Who does Ivan help on his family's farm?
   6 What time does Ivan get up every day?

3   Ivan lives on a goat farm in France. They get milk from their goats to make goat cheese and sell it. Ivan helps look after the goats. Every morning, he has to get up at 5 o'clock. He helps his father feed the goats and get the milk. He goes to school after he does his chores. "I like helping my dad," he says.

4   Chen Wei's mother makes the best noodles and people come to her shop from all over Singapore to eat them. The work can be very tiring for one person only so after he does his homework, Chen Wei helps his mother cook noodles. "I love eating noodles too!" he says.

5   It's great to help, isn't it?

28 **Look at 26. Play a game.**

1 feed animals
2 help my mum cook
3 shovel the snow off our car
4 wash the empty bowls
5 wear warm gloves
6 help my father make cheese

I have to feed animals.

You're Ivan!

29 **Ask your classmates what chores they have to do to help their family. Make a list. Look at this example:**

What chores do you have to do to help your family?

Total number of people in class: 12

1 clean their room   10 out of 12
2 walk the dog   7 out of 12
3 ….

I clean my room.

 **THINK BIG** **Which chores look difficult and which look easy? Why?**

30 Find the words we **don't** capitalise in the titles.

> Use capital letters for most words in titles.
> Taking Care of a Big Dog

Good Things to Eat

My Brother and I

The Big Blue Car

A Day at the Park with Grandma

To the Moon and Back

31 Rewrite the titles. Use capital letters where necessary.

1 helping my dad
2 lots of chores for my brother
3 helping out around the house
4 a strange day out
5 the jobs I like
6 helping my family is fun
7 my sister's new job

32 How many English titles do you know?
Write them with a partner.

33 **Listen, read and repeat.**

1 ay   **2** oy

 34 **Listen and find. Then say.**

May

t**oy**

35 **Listen and blend the sounds.**

1 d-ay   day   **2** j-oy   joy
3 s-ay   say   **4** p-ay   pay
5 b-oy   boy   **6** s-oy   soy
7 w-ay   way   **8** r-ay   ray

36 **Read aloud. Then listen and chant.**

What do we say?
It's May, it's May,
It's a nice day.
Come on, girls!
Come on, boys!
Bring your toys.

37 Look and listen. Are they happy to help? Say **yes** or **no**.

64

1

2

38 Role play the dialogues in **37** with a partner.

PROJECT

39 Make a sock puppet. With a partner, use your puppet to role play helping someone.

40 **Read and match. Then make statements for you. Use the words from the box.**

> always   have to   never   sometimes   usually

1 study for	**a** dog
2 do	**b** the piano
3 clean	**c** my room
4 walk the	**d** a test
5 practise	**e** the dishes

41 **Copy the chart in your notebook and complete for you. Then ask and answer.**

My Chores	Mon	Tue	Wed	Thu	Fri	Sat	Sun
clean my room							
do my homework							
do the dishes							
study for a test							

> Do you always clean your room?

> No, I don't. I always do my homework.

42 **Read and complete.**

1 They don't like ❓ football. (play)

2 He loves ❓ people's photos. (take)

3 She hates ❓ a bike. (ride)

4 You like ❓ juice. (drink)

5 I love ❓ in the sea. (swim)

I Can

- talk about how often people do things.
- talk about what people like/don't like doing and have to do.
- talk about chores and pocket money.
- use capital letters in titles.

How Well Do I Know It? Can I Use It?

1 **Think about it. Read and draw. Practise.**

😊 I know this.   😐 I need more practice.   😟 I don't know this.

		PAGES			
1	**Daily activities:** eat breakfast, go to school, practise the piano…	4, 36	😊	😐	😟
2	**Telling time:** one o'clock, two thirty, 5:15…	5	😊	😐	😟
3	**Jobs:** cashier, firefighter, nurse…	20	😊	😐	😟
4	**Workplaces:** police station, restaurant, shop…	21	😊	😐	😟
5	**When** does she get dressed? She gets dressed **at 7:00 in the morning**.	8	😊	😐	😟
6	What does he do **before** school? He eats breakfast **before** school. I watch TV **after** school.	9	😊	😐	😟
7	They **always/usually/sometimes/never** do their homework after school.	12, 41	😊	😐	😟
8	What **does** he **do**? He **is** a cashier. Where **does** he **work**? He **works** at a shop.	24–25	😊	😐	😟
9	**Does** he **swim**? Yes, he **does**. I **play** music. I **don't do** sports.	28–29	😊	😐	😟
10	What **do** they **have to** do? They **have to** feed the fish.	40	😊	😐	😟
11	I/You/They **like/love/hate** cleaning. He/She/It **likes/loves/hates** swimming.	44–45	😊	😐	😟

65

2 **Get ready.**

A Complete the interview. Use the words from the box.
Then listen and check.

> Do you eat dinner at home?
> usually
> What do you do?
> What do you do before work?
> When do you go to work?
> Where do you work?

Katy: [1] ?

Max: I'm a chef.

Katy: Oh, really? [2] ?

Max: I work at a restaurant,
the Pizza Palace.

Katy: I see. [3] ?

Max: I [4] ? go to work at 2:00. I come home at 11:00 at night.

Katy: OK. [5] ?

Max: I have a shower, eat breakfast and get dressed. Then I
feed my fish.

Katy: [6] ?

Max: No, I always eat dinner at the restaurant.

B Make more questions.

1 When ? ?

2 ? before work?

3 ? in the afternoon?

C Practise the dialogue in **A** with a partner. Include your new questions.

3 **Get set.**

 **STEP 1** Choose a job.

 **STEP 2** Write notes about your daily routine.

 **STEP 3** Cut out the cards on page 157 of your Activity Book. Now you're ready to **GO!**

Me

I'm a(n) _____ .

I work at _____ .

I usually _____ every day.

4 **Go!**

A Use the cards to make questions. Interview your partner. Write about your partner's daily routine. Then switch roles.

My partner's day

He's/She's a(n) _____ .

He/She works at _____ .

He/She _____ every day.

B Work in groups. Tell your classmates about your partner's daily routine.

Luisa always eats breakfast before school.

5 Write about yourself in your notebook.

- When do you wake up?
- What do you do before school?
- What chores do you have to do?

- What do you like doing after school?
- What time do you go to bed?
- What chores do you never do?

How Well Do I Know It Now?

6 Think about it. Look at page **52** and your notebook. Draw again.

A Use a different colour.

B Read and think.

I can start the next unit.

I can ask my teacher for help and then start the next unit.

I can practise and then start the next unit.

7 Rate this Checkpoint.

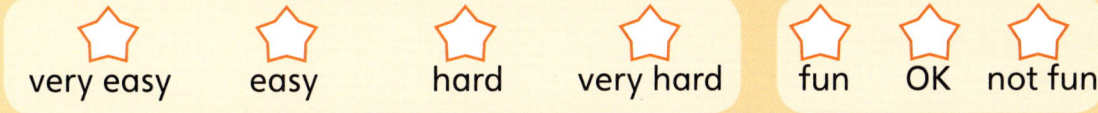

very easy   easy   hard   very hard   fun   OK   not fun

– Part A –

66

Listen and write. There is one example.

My dad's farm

Name of farm: <u>Happy Farm</u>

1 Where?   near the _____

2 How many chickens: _____

3 Colour of cow: _____

4 Dog's name: _____

5 What time starts work?   _____ in the morning

Read the story. Choose a word from the box. Write the correct word next to numbers 1–6. There is one example.

My name is Charlie. My mum and dad are _____nurses_____. They work at the

(1) _____. They usually work in the morning but sometimes they start work

in the evening. They have to wear a white uniform.

When my (2) _____ work in the evening, my grandma and grandad come

to our house. I play video (3) _____ with my grandad. He's very good!

My grandma always makes dinner and I take out the (4) _____. Then we

(5) _____ TV for an hour and I go to my room. In the morning, my

grandma always tells me "Make your (6) _____ before you go!"

Example

nurses	games	restaurant	parents	bed
play	watch	hospital	rubbish	

---

(7) Now choose the best name for the story.

   Check (✓) one box.

   Charlie's video games ⬜

   My mum is a nurse ⬜

   Grandparents always help ⬜

unit 4 Amazing Animals

67

1 **Listen, look and say.**

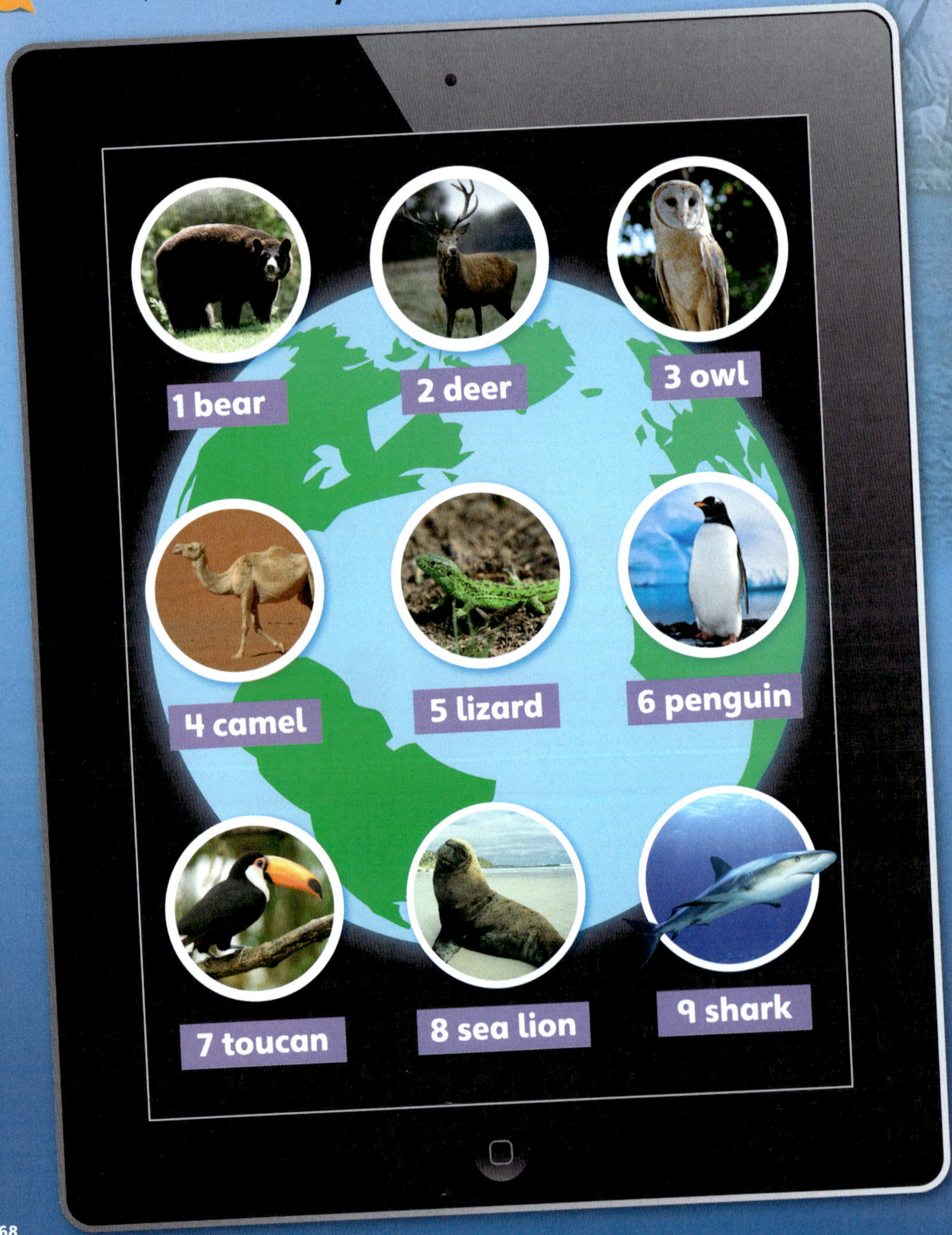
1 bear
2 deer
3 owl
4 camel
5 lizard
6 penguin
7 toucan
8 sea lion
9 shark

68

2 **Listen, find and say.**

3 **Play a game.**

16 **Look at 15. Read and match.**

1 Camouflage helps animals
2 Polar bears are covered in white fur to
3 Chameleons can
4 Stonefish wait for their food to
5 Grey tree frogs
6 Birds and snakes

a come to them.
b live in forests.
c blend in with the snow.
d hide from other animals.
e hunt for grey tree frogs.
f change their colour.

17 **Complete the fact cards.**

name:
chameleon
found:
❓
camouflage:
❓

name:
❓
found:
forests
camouflage:
❓

name:
❓
found:
❓
camouflage:
looks like snow

name:
❓
found:
bottom of the sea
camouflage:
❓

PROJECT

18 **Make four cards like the ones in 17. Write about the animals in the list or use your own ideas. Then play a game.**

snowy owls
stick insects
octopus
leopards

It's found in trees. It looks like a small branch of a tree.

It's a stick insect!

Well done! You get one point.

78

19 **Look, listen and read. Are they hungry?**

Dog: Woof! Our humans are having a party!

Cat: Shhh! Walk quietly!

Dog: Look at those burgers! Can we eat them?

Cat: OK, but can you run fast?

quiet	quiet**ly**
slow	slow**ly**
easy	easi**ly**
careful	careful**ly**

	But...
good	**well**
fast	**fast**
hard	**hard**
far	**far**

She works very **hard**.
Can he run **fast**?
I don't feel **well**.

20 **Read, match and complete.**

1 Amanda is slow.
2 You are a fast eater.
3 David is loud.
4 Fred is a good artist.
5 My mum's a careful driver.
6 I'm a bad cook.

a She drives ❓.
b He can paint very ❓.
c You eat ❓.
d She walks ❓.
e I cook ❓.
f He speaks ❓.

21 **Read and complete. Use the words from the box.**

> carefully   easily   far   fast   hard   well

1 I work very ❓ at school.
2 Big cats can run very ❓.
3 Don't push the door. It opens ❓.
4 Please cross the road ❓.
5 I know him very ❓. He's my best friend.
6 We don't have to walk ❓. The house is over there.

22 **Look at the chart. Read and make a list in your notebook.**

1 Adnan is a quiet child.
2 She's playing very badly today.
3 I have to study hard for this test.
4 It's a very good film.
5 You're walking very fast!
6 You have to be careful at work.

quiet	badly

23 **Read and choose.**

1 I can read Italian but I can't speak very **good/well** yet.
2 This place is very **noisy/noisily**!
3 Eat your food **slow/slowly**.
4 You have to speak **quiet/quietly** in the library.
5 Let's finish **quick/quickly**! We don't have time.
6 The music isn't very **loud/loudly**.

24 **Read and complete for you.**

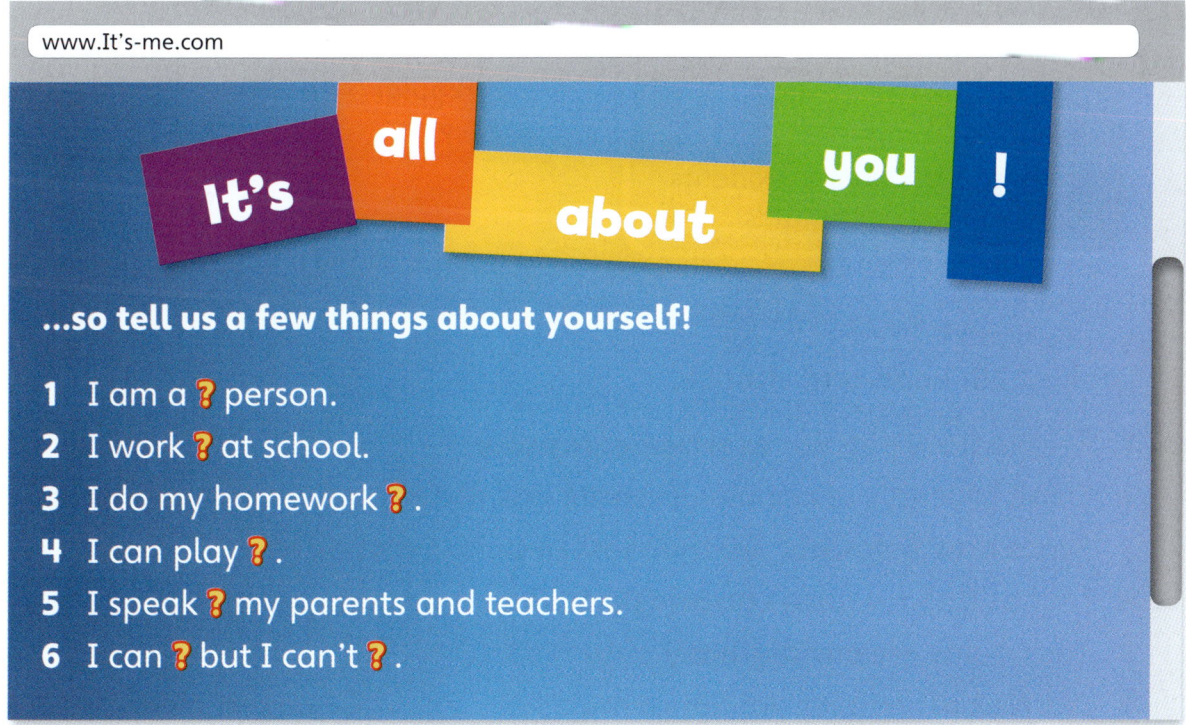

www.It's-me.com

It's all about you !

...so tell us a few things about yourself!

1 I am a **?** person.
2 I work **?** at school.
3 I do my homework **?** .
4 I can play **?** .
5 I speak **?** my parents and teachers.
6 I can **?** but I can't **?** .

Pets in Different Places

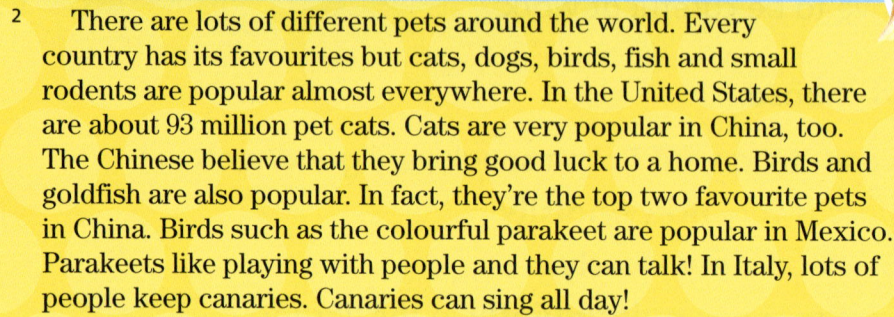

1   Many people around the world keep pets. Pets are good company but they also help us in other ways. We get exercise when we take our dogs for a walk. They also keep us safe. Cats keep mice and big insects away from our homes. Our pets help us relax and we love playing with them or just watching them!

2   There are lots of different pets around the world. Every country has its favourites but cats, dogs, birds, fish and small rodents are popular almost everywhere. In the United States, there are about 93 million pet cats. Cats are very popular in China, too. The Chinese believe that they bring good luck to a home. Birds and goldfish are also popular. In fact, they're the top two favourite pets in China. Birds such as the colourful parakeet are popular in Mexico. Parakeets like playing with people and they can talk! In Italy, lots of people keep canaries. Canaries can sing all day!

25 Why do you think people keep animals as pets? Make a list of reasons as a class.

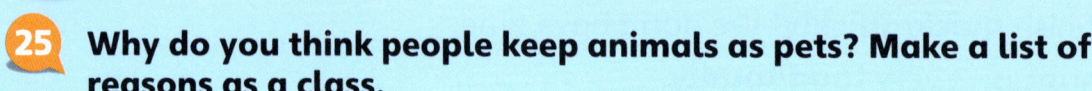

79
26 Listen and read. Check your answers in 25. Then complete the chart.

CONTENT WORDS
alligators   canaries   geckos
goldfish   parakeets   rodents
snakes   tarantulas

Popular pets	Unusual pets	Dangerous pets
❓	❓	❓

27 Look at 26. Read and choose.

1   People have pets for **exercise/company**.

2   Small rodents are popular in **some countries only/many countries**.

3   **Birds and fish/Cats** are the most popular pets in China.

4   Lots of Italians have **canaries/parakeets** as pets.

5   Tarantulas are **cuddly/easy** pets.

6   **All/Not all** reptiles are dangerous.

3 One of Japan's popular pets is the bunny rabbit. There are even bunny cafés, where you can have a coffee and spend time with these furry animals or buy one!

4 Some people choose unusual or exotic pets. Chilean Rose Hair Tarantulas are quiet and easy to keep but they aren't very cuddly. They don't usually bite but if they do, it can be painful! There are millions of reptile pet owners around the world. Reptiles such as iguanas or geckos aren't dangerous but snakes or alligators can be very dangerous so pet owners need to be extra careful.

5 There's a type of pet for everyone. People all over the world choose different pets for different reasons. One thing is important, though. Our pets are our friends and they need our love and care.

 Work with a partner. Discuss which pet is best for each person.

Ethan
-is often away from home
-lives in a very small flat

Isabella
-wants a colourful pet
-loves talking to animals

Jed
-is allergic to animal fur
-wants an unusual pet

Sandra
-lives in a big flat
-likes staying at home

How about a hamster for Ethan?

I don't think so. He's often away from home. Hamsters need feeding every day.

 **THINK BIG** **Some people keep wild animals as pets. Do you agree?**

81

29 **Listen and read. What's Spotty like?**

title ⟶

topic
sentence ⟶

My Favourite Pet

by Aaron Michaels

My favourite pet is my snake, Spotty. He is a corn snake. He is 50 centimetres long and he is red and white. I feed him one small mouse every week. He is friendly. He does not bite people. Some people don't like snakes but snakes can make good pets.

30 **Read 26 again. Find the first topic sentence.**

> A topic sentence gives the main idea in a paragraph.

31 **Read and match the titles to the topic sentences.**

Title	Topic Sentence
1 A Day at the Zoo	**a** My sister and I have got many pets at home.
2 My Mother's Job	**b** My favourite time of day at school is Art class.
3 My Favourite Class	**c** I have to do lots of chores at home after school.
4 After-School Jobs	**d** My mother is a chef at an Italian restaurant.
5 Our Pets	**e** When I go to the zoo, I spend the whole day there.

32 **What is your favourite animal? Write a title and a topic sentence.**

82
 33 **Listen, read and repeat.**

1 **ea**   2 **oi**   3 **oe**

83
 34 **Listen and find. Then say.**

  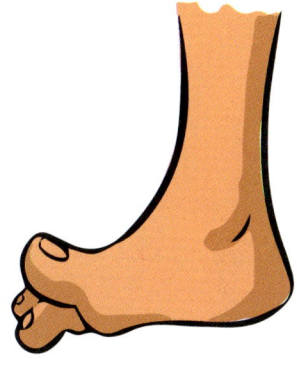

eat   c**oi**n   t**oe**

84
 **35** **Listen and blend the sounds.**

1 s-ea   sea   2 b-oi-l   boil
3 b-ea-n   bean   4 t-ea   tea
5 p-ea-ch   peach   6 m-ea-t   meat
7 oi-l   oil   8 f-oe   foe

85
 36 **Read aloud. Then listen and chant.**

So, Joe, boil the beans,
Add the oil,
Add the meat.
Eat the beans,
Eat the meat,
Eat the peach
And drink the tea.

Values | Protect animals and their habitats.

37 **Look at the map of animals in Australia. Play a game.**

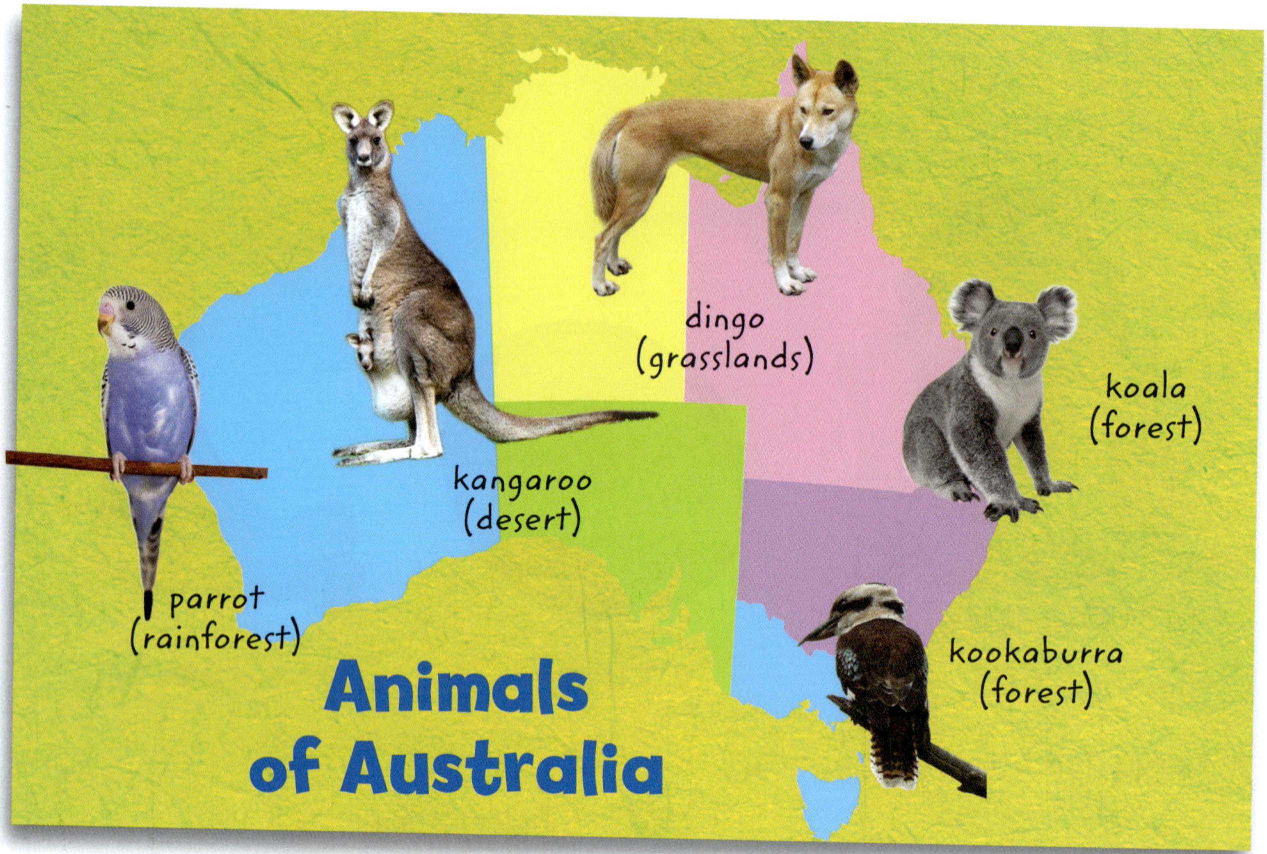
Animals of Australia
dingo (grasslands)
kangaroo (desert)
koala (forest)
parrot (rainforest)
kookaburra (forest)

Parrots in Australia live in the desert.

Wrong! They live in rainforests.

PROJECT

38 **Work in a group. Make an Animals Map.**

- Choose a continent.
- Research the animals that live there.
- Draw and label your part of the map.

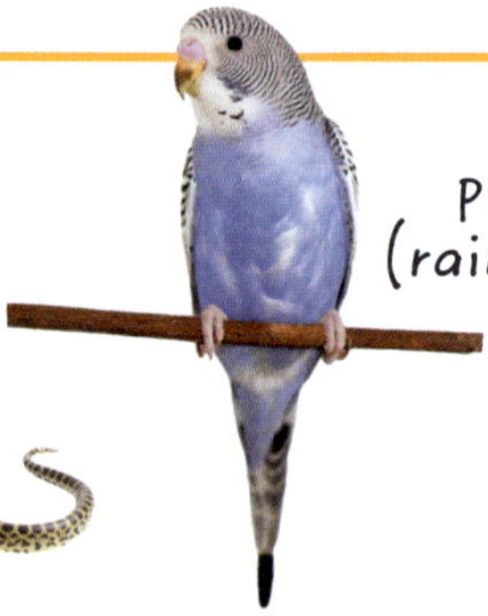
parrot (rainforest)

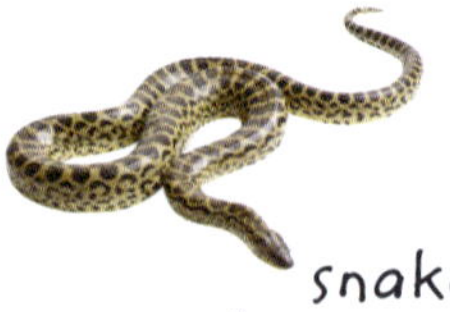
snake (rainforest)

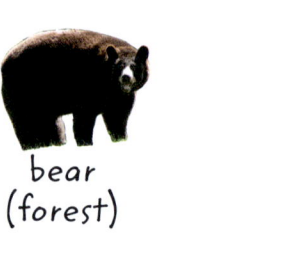

bear (forest)

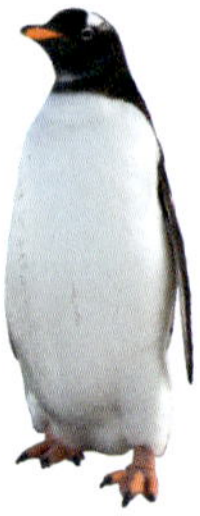
penguin (ice and snow)

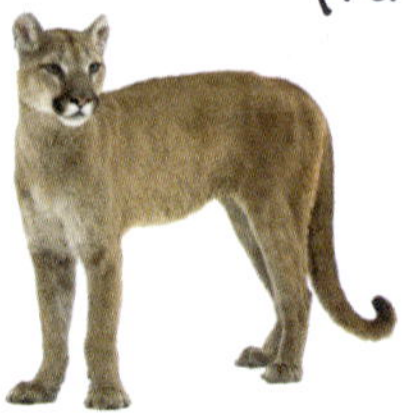
mountain lion (mountains)

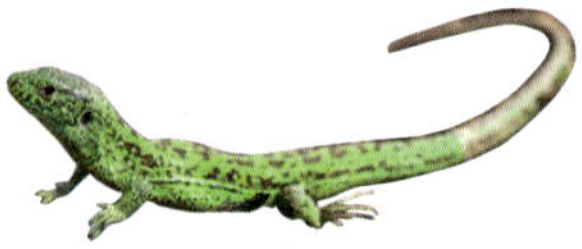
lizard (rainforest)

39 **Complete the sentences. Use the correct form of the words from the box.**

bad   careful   easy   good   hard   slow

1   Turtles walk very ❓ .
2   He always studies very ❓ .
3   Watch out! You should play ❓ .
4   The choir is great. They sing ❓ .
5   Sorry, I can't help you. I draw really ❓ .
6   I did really well! I answered all the questions ❓ .

40 **Complete the dialogue. Then ask and answer.**

Daniel: Where do sharks live?
Teresa: ¹ ❓ .
Daniel: Right. ² ❓
Teresa: Camels live in the desert.
Daniel: Right again! ³ ❓
Teresa: Camels can walk and run a little but they can't jump or fly.
Daniel: How about penguins? Can they swim and fly?
Teresa: ⁴ ❓
Daniel: That's right!

41 **Make sentences about toucans and sea lions.**

What can they do?
What can't they do?
Where are they found?

I Can

- talk about what animals can/can't do and where they're found.
- find and use adverbs.
- find and use topic sentences.

unit 5 Wonderful Weather!

1 Listen, look and say. [87]

1 It's windy.

2 It's cold and snowy.

The Weather today

- hot
- warm
- cool
- cold

3 It's cool and cloudy.

4 It's hot and sunny.

5 It's warm and rainy.

2 Listen, find and say. [88]

3 Play a game.

4  **89 90** Listen and sing. What's the weather like today?

Cool Weekend!

What's the weather like today?
Rainy, sunny, hot or cold?

On Sunday, it was rainy,
It was very cold, too.
I was nice and warm in my winter coat,
Outside the sky wasn't blue!

Now it's Monday. It's sunny.
Great! I can go out and play.
Oh, no! I have to go to school.
Never mind! The weekend was cool!

Chorus (x2)

5 **91** Listen and find. Then ask and answer for you.

a — sunglasses, sandals, shorts

b — jumper, scarf

c — raincoat

d — coat

What do you wear on sunny days?

On sunny days, I wear shorts, a T-shirt and sunglasses.

THINK BIG What weather is good for...
a football practice? **b** a walk in the park?
c going to the beach? **d** going skiing?

 song/vocabulary (clothes) Unit 5 **75**

93

6 **Listen and read. Where is Amy going today?**

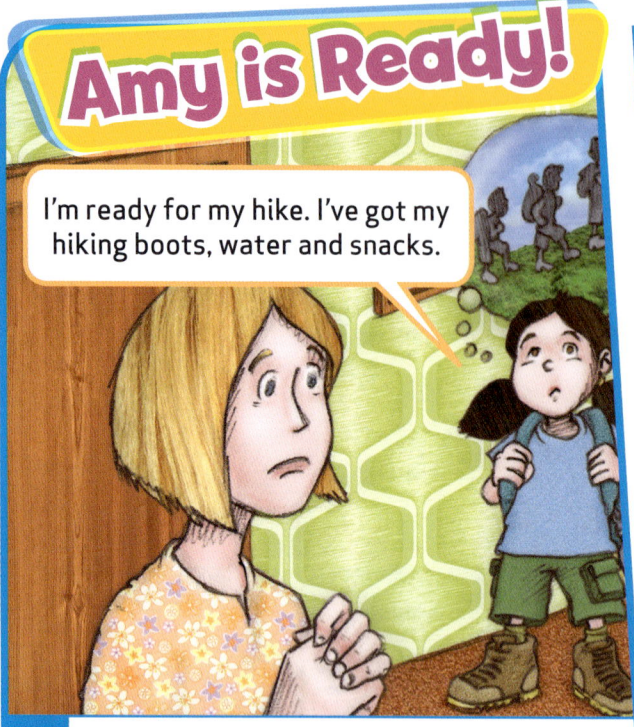

1 Amy is happy. Today her class is going on a hike.

2 Mum doesn't think Amy is ready.

3 Mum doesn't want Amy to get wet.

4 She doesn't want Amy to get cold.

5 Amy isn't worried about the weather.

6 Amy is ready for all kinds of weather!

7 **Look at the story. Answer the questions with a partner.**

1 What's Amy's class doing today?

2 What was the weather like yesterday?

3 What was the weather like last night?

4 What's the weather like today?

5 What's Amy wearing at the end of the story?

THINK BIG **Do you think it's a good idea for Amy to take so many clothes?**
What clothes would you take?

94

8 Listen and look at the sentences. Help Luke and Amy make more.

cold   windy   cloudy

What   is   the weather like   today   ?

It   's   warm and sunny   now   .

What   was   the weather like   yesterday   ?

It   was   rainy and cold   .

I   wasn't   hot   .

We   weren't   warm   last Sunday   .

9 Look at the weather chart. Answer the questions.

M	T	W	Th	F

1 Today is Monday. What's the weather like today?
2 Today is Tuesday. What's the weather like today?
3 It's sunny. What day is it today?
4 It's windy. What day is it today?
5 Today is Thursday. What was the weather like yesterday?

10 Ask and answer.

I'm wearing a T-shirt, shorts and sandals. What's the weather like?

It's sunny and warm.

11 **Read and find the correct sentence and say. Correct for you.**

1 It is sunny yesterday.
It was sunny yesterday.

2 Today it's snowy.
Yesterday it's snowy.

3 It's cool and windy now.
It was cool and windy now.

4 It was rainy last night.
It is rainy last night.

5 We aren't warm last Sunday.
We weren't warm last Sunday.

6 She isn't cold today.
She wasn't cold today.

It wasn't sunny yesterday.

12 **Complete the roleplay with _is_ or _was_. Then say with your partner.**

Derya: My holiday is great fun. Yesterday, ¹ [?] great! I ² [?] at the beach all day!

George: Wow! What ³ [?] the weather like yesterday?

Derya: It ⁴ [?] hot and sunny. What ⁵ [?] the weather like at home today?

George: It ⁶ [?] cool and rainy.

13 **Put the temperatures in order. Start with cold. Make sentences about what you are wearing.**

cold   cool   hot   warm

It's cold today. I'm wearing boots, trousers, a jumper, coat and gloves.

14 What's your favourite type of weather? Discuss as a class.

96

15 Listen and read. Then match.

CONTENT WORDS
average   climate   degrees Celsius
desert   dry   extreme   mild   minus

Changing Climates

1   The year-round weather in a place is called climate. It isn't the same for every place on the planet and it usually changes with the seasons. In Southern Europe, for example, winters are usually mild. It often rains but it doesn't snow much. Summers are generally dry and warm. In some places, however, the climate is the same all year long – and it can be extreme.

2   The Lut Desert in Iran is very hot and dry all year round. The temperatures there can be 70 degrees Celsius! Because of the extreme temperatures, some parts of the Lut desert have no life at all. Now you know why not many people go there! The Atacama Desert in Chile, on the other hand, is very popular with tourists. The temperatures are mild all year round but in some parts of this desert, it never rains at all. People say the Atacama Desert looks like the moon and they love its natural beauty.

3   If it never rains in the Altacama Desert, it rains almost every day in Lloró, Colombia. Lloró gets an average of 13 metres of rain every year. That's a lot! The trees grow very quickly because of the wet climate.

4   In Oymyakon, Russia, winters are very long and cold. It snows all the time and temperatures can be minus 70 degrees Celsius. If you think that snow means no school, you're wrong. Schools close only when the temperature is below minus 52 degrees Celsius!

5   Places with a good climate are very popular. But lots of sun and high temperatures isn't everyone's idea of a good climate. Some people really like the cold or wet weather. So long as everyone's happy!

1 Southern Europe	**a** No rain.
2 Lut Desert, Iran	**b** Extreme cold.
3 Atacama Desert, Chile	**c** Lots of rain.
4 Lloró, Colombia	**d** Mild winters.
5 Oymyakon, Russia	**e** Very hot and dry.

THINK BIG What difficulties do people who live in extreme climates have?

16 Look at **15**. Correct the mistakes.

1 The whole planet has got the same climate.
2 It usually snows in Southern Europe in winter.
3 There's no life in the Lut Desert at all.
4 The Atacama Desert doesn't have many visitors.
5 Lloró and the Atacama Desert have the same climate.
6 Schools in Oymyakon close only when it's below minus 70 degrees Celsius.

17 Complete the chart with information about the climate where you live. Use the chart to ask and answer with a partner.

Place	Climate	Weather	Effect
desert	hot and dry	never rains	not many plants grow there
rainforest	hot and wet	rains all the time	there are lots of plants and trees
high mountains	cold and snowy	snows a lot	they're great places for skiing
?	?	?	?

 What's the weather like in the desert?

It's hot and dry. It never rains in the desert. That's why not many plants grow there.

PROJECT

18 Choose one of the places in the list and make a **Climate** poster. Then present it to the class.

The Amazon Rainforest
The Sahara Desert
The Mediterranean
The Andean Mountain Range

The Canadian Arctic is very cold and snowy. In winter, temperatures can be minus 50 degrees Celsius. As a result, many animals sleep all winter.

Grammar

19 Look and read. Then say.

a   b

What was your holiday like? Was it hot and sunny? The weather was great here!

It wasn't sunny and it wasn't hot. It was rainy and it was miserable. There wasn't a nice beach and there wasn't a swimming pool.

Oh! Were there nice shops?

Yes, there were fantastic shops but they weren't open!

I/He/She/It		**was**	late.
You/We/They		**were**	early.
I/He/She/It		**wasn't**	in the desert.
You/We/They		**weren't**	freezing.
Was	I/he/she/it	thirsty?	Yes, I/he/she/it **was**. No, I/he/she/it **wasn't**.
Were	you/we/they	hungry?	Yes, you/we/they **were**. Yes, you/we/they **weren't**.

There **was**	a turtle in the zoo.
Was **there**	any water?
There **wasn't**	cake on the table.
There **were**	umbrellas on the chair.

20 Read and choose.

1 Albert Einstein **was/were** from Germany.

2 Michael Jackson **was/were** a singer.

3 There **was/were** ice on the River Thames last winter.

4 There **was/were** seven dwarfs in the fairytale *Snow White*.

5 The Olympic Games **was/were** in London in 2012.

6 The first people on the moon **was/were** American.

21 **Make true sentences for you. Use was/wasn't or were/weren't.**

1 It ❓ Sunday yesterday.

2 We ❓ at the beach on Saturday.

3 I ❓ hungry at 9 o' clock.

4 My friends ❓ at my house yesterday.

5 The weather ❓ bad yesterday.

6 Our dinner ❓ yummy yesterday.

22 **Put the words in order. Then say.**

1 | with your family | you | last weekend? | Were |

2 | were | Where | night? | last | you |

3 | you | fifteen | Were | on your last birthday? |

4 | hot | it | Was | a | yesterday? | day |

5 | Was | a film | on TV | there | last night? |

6 | Were | your | and raincoat | umbrella | bag | in your | yesterday? |

23 **Think about two things from the past or choose from the list. Discuss with a partner.**

- your last school (teacher, classroom, pupils, playground, friends, lessons)
- the weather last summer (rainy, sunny, cold, hot, windy)
- your town a hundred years ago (shops, big/small, people, houses, parks)

My last school was nice. There were three teachers and the classroom was big. There were twenty pupils. There was a cool playground. Our lessons were easy. My friends were Katie, Adam and Jamie.

All Weather Fun

Children around the world enjoy outdoor sports and activities. In the United States, many children play baseball. In India and England, cricket and field hockey are popular. And, of course, children all over the world play football. But when the weather is bad, it isn't much fun to play any of these sports. So what can you do? Wear the right clothes and make the weather work for you. Here are some ideas.

1 ❓

If it's too windy, it can be difficult to play football or other outdoor ball sports. But a windy day is great for flying a kite. Children all over the world enjoy flying kites but it's a very popular activity in Japan and other Asian countries. It's even more fun if you make the kite yourself. It's very easy and you can find all the information on the Internet!

24 **Are these sports and activities usually indoor or outdoor? Which can be both? Discuss with a partner.**

| football | basketball | bowling | skateboarding | table tennis |
| skiing | volleyball | field hockey | baseball | swimming |

98

25 **Listen and read. Match the titles A–C to paragraphs 1–3.**

> **CONTENT WORDS**
> cricket   fill up   kite
> sledging   snow fight

A No umbrellas, please!
B Put on your woolly hats and gloves!
C Hold on tight!

26 **Look at 25. Read and say true or false.**

1 Baseball is very popular in India.
2 You can't play all outdoor sports on windy days.
3 It's easy to make a kite.
4 In parts of Africa, it rains all year round.
5 You can ride a sledge with or without a dog.
6 Pulling a sledge isn't fun for dogs.

2 ❓

Rain doesn't stop African children from having fun. In parts of Africa, it's dry for many months of the year. But when the rain comes, the dry rivers and lakes fill up quickly. Kids love it. They go swimming and play games in the water. It's a fun time for everyone when it rains.

3 ❓

Having fun in the snow is easy. Everyone loves snow fights and building snowmen. In Alaska and parts of Canada, where it snows a lot, kids often go sledging. Some kids also do an interesting sport called dog sledging. Dogs pull the sledge and the kids ride on it. The dogs and the kids love it!

So next time the weather is bad, don't stay in and watch TV. Even if it's windy, wet or cold, there are lots of fun things to do outside.

27 **Ask and answer with a partner.**

skiing	between -1 and -6 degrees Celsius, clear sky
wind surfing	windy, sunny or cloudy
football	any kind of weather except extreme weather
sea swimming	hot, sunny
rock climbing	warm, not very windy

What's the best weather for skiing?

When the temperature is between -1 and -6 degrees Celsius and the sky is clear.

THINK BIG **How many outdoor sports and activities can you think of? Make a list.**

28 **Read. Then choose.**

Here is a topic sentence.

My favourite season is summer.

After the topic sentence, we give more information with detail sentences.

In the summer where I live, the weather is usually sunny and hot. I like going to the beach with my friends. We swim or play volleyball.

detail sentence   topic sentence

1 A ❓ tells us what the paragraph is about.

2 A ❓ gives us more information.

29 **Read the topic sentence below. Which sentences give details about this topic?**

Topic sentence: *Winter is my favourite time of year.*

1 We like building snowmen in winter, too.

2 It's not cold in summer.

3 My friends and I like to go sledging.

4 We usually wear hats and gloves in winter.

5 My sister's favourite season is spring.

6 It's cold and snowy in winter but I like it.

Writing Steps

30 **Write about your favourite season.**

1 Choose your favourite season.

2 Write a title.

3 Write a topic sentence.

4 Write three detail sentences.

 **31** **100** **Listen, read and repeat.**

1 **sc**   2 **sw**   3 **sn**   4 **sl**

 **32** **101** **Listen and find. Then say.**

scarf   **sw**eet   **sn**ail   **sl**eep

 33 **102** **Listen and blend the sounds.**

1 s-c-ou-t   scout   2 s-n-a-ck   snack
3 s-w-i-m   swim   4 s-l-i-m   slim
5 s-n-ow   snow   6 s-w-a-n   swan
7 s-l-ow   slow   8 s-c-ar   scar

 **34** **103** **Read aloud. Then listen and chant.**

A slow snail is eating a snack
And a slim swan is swimming.

105

35 Look, listen and point.

a

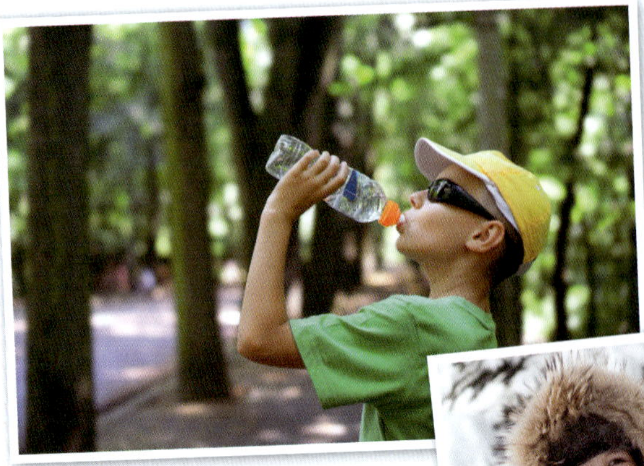

b

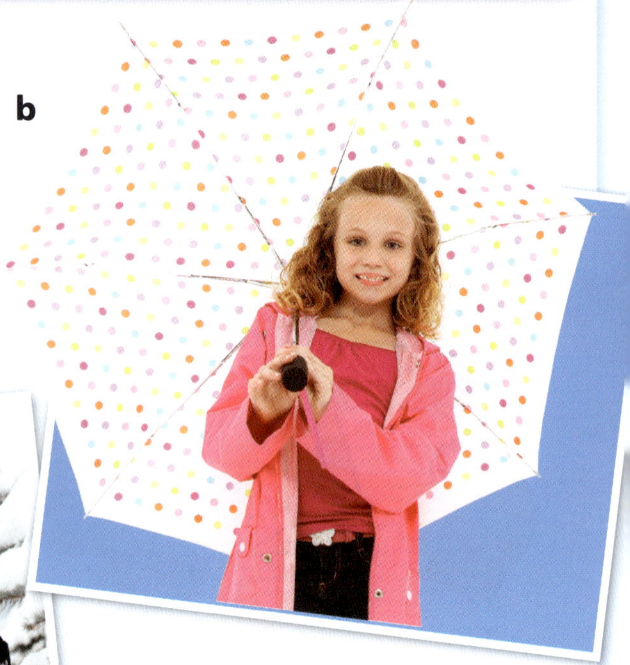

c

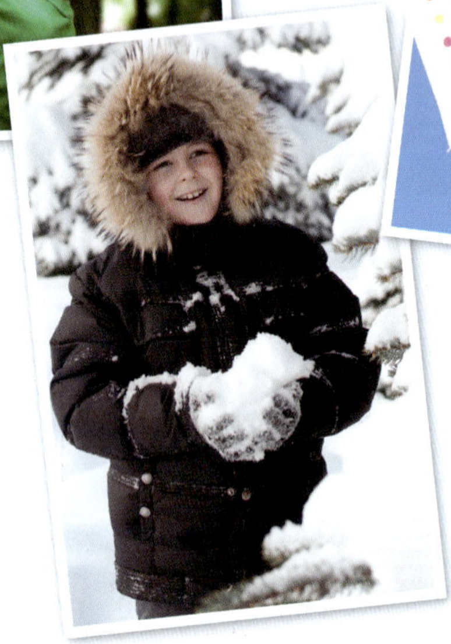

PROJECT

36 Work with a group. Make a **Prepare for the Weather** checklist.

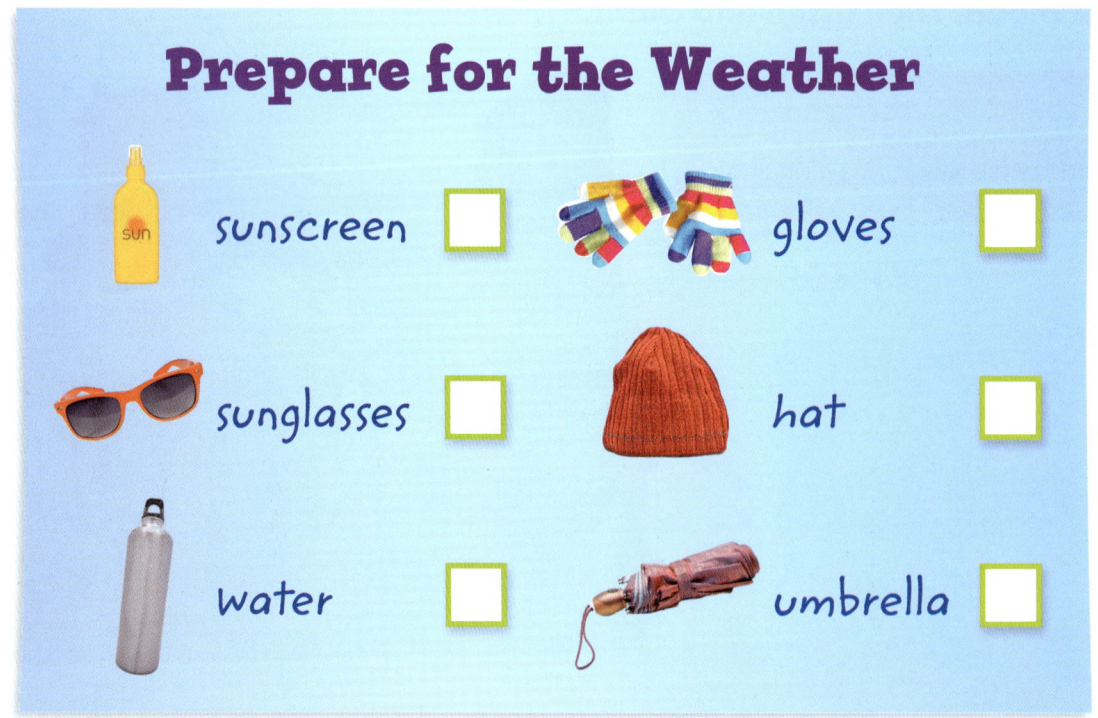

Prepare for the Weather

sunscreen ☐

gloves ☐

sunglasses ☐

hat ☐

water ☐

umbrella ☐

37 Look at the weather reports. Complete the questions and answers.

Barcelona, Spain	
Yesterday	Today

Temperature: 33 °C	Temperature: 28 °C

Glasgow, Scotland	
Yesterday	Today
Temperature: 4 °C	Temperature: 12 °C

1 What/weather/Barcelona/yesterday?

3 What/weather/Barcelona/today?

5 What/weather/Glasgow/yesterday?

7 What/weather/Glasgow/today?

2 Yesterday, in Barcelona it was ❓ .

4 Today, it's ❓ .

6 ❓

8 ❓

38 Find the differences. Talk with a partner.

Picture 1

Picture 2

In Picture 1, it's hot and sunny.

In Picture 2, it's cold and snowy.

39 Choose one picture from **38**. Write a topic sentence and three detail sentences.

I Can

- talk about the weather today and in the past.
- talk about clothes.
- talk about climates around the world.
- find and use detail sentences.

unit 6 Smells Good!

1 **Listen, look and say.**

1 This music sounds lovely.

2 This band sounds awful.

3 This soup tastes horrible.

4 This pie tastes delicious.

Senses

5 This apple tastes sweet.

6 These flowers smell nice.

7 My hair looks terrible.

8 My jumper feels soft.

9 These shoes feel tight.

2 **Listen, find and say.**

3 **Play a game.**

4 Listen and sing. Where do the girls like going?

Grandma's House

We love my Grandma's house.
It always smells so nice.
It smells like ginger cookies
Sweet, with a little spice!

**Yummy smells and her smiling face.
We really love my Grandma's place.**

Grandma likes playing old songs
From when she was very young.
The music sounds so wonderful,
We have to sing along.

We always do my favourite thing
Baking ginger cookies.
They taste so nice and yummy,
We are both very lucky!

Chorus

5 Match the pictures to the words. Then ask and answer about 1.

feel
look
smell
sound
taste

This pie tastes delicious.

Number 4.

THINK BIG Can you think of other things you describe with these adjectives?
sweet   tight   lovely   horrible

Story

 6 **Listen and read. What kind of soup does Luke try?**

1 Luke smells something bad coming from the kitchen.

2 It *is* fish soup. Luke thinks it smells horrible.

3 Amy tries the soup.

4 Luke tries the soup.

> Yuck! It tastes terrible!

5 | Luke thinks the soup tastes awful.

> Sorry, I've got a cold... achoo! I can't smell or taste anything!

6 | Amy has got a cold. That's why she can't taste the soup.

7 Put the sentences in order.

a   Amy thinks the soup tastes OK.

b   Luke thinks the soup tastes terrible.

c   Luke thinks the fish soup smells awful.

d   Amy tries the soup.

e   Luke tries the soup.

f   Luke asks Amy to try the soup.

THINK BIG **Which senses do we use when we are...**
a in a restaurant?   b at a football match?
c at school?

How do our senses make us aware of danger?

112

8 Listen and look at the sentences. Help Luke and Amy make more.

sound | look | smell

horrible | OK | nice

How | does | the soup taste | ?

It | tastes | delicious | .

How | do | the sandals feel | ?

They | feel | tight | .

113

9 Are the adjectives positive or negative? Copy and complete. Then listen and check.

amazing awful bad delicious good horrible lovely nice terrible

Positive	Negative
amazing	awful

10 **Read and choose. Complete the answers.**

awful   good   great   nice   soft

1 A: How do these flowers **smell/smells**?

B: ❓ .

2 A: How does my new shirt **look/looks**?

B: ❓ . I like the colour.

3 A: How does the sandwich **taste/tastes**?

B: ❓ . I don't like tomatoes!

4 A: How does the school band **sound/sounds**?

B: ❓ . They practise every day.

5 A: How do your new gloves **feel/feels**?

B: ❓ .

11 **Complete the questions.**

1 ❓ the guitar music sound?

2 ❓ the flowers smell?

3 ❓ my hair look today?

4 ❓ that pizza taste?

5 ❓ the shoes feel?

12 **Ask and answer. Use the words from the boxes.**

delicious   great   horrible   lovely   soft   tight

apples   flowers   hat   music   trousers

 How does the music sound?

It sounds lovely.

13 Discuss with a partner.

1 How may senses do you think we've got: 4, 5 or 6?

2 What sense do we use these parts of the body for?

a fingers b nose c eyes d ears e tongue f feet g brain

115
14 Listen and read. Then check your answers in **13**.

CONTENT WORDS

avoid   brain   danger   echo   information
senses   sound waves   taste buds   tongue

Our Senses Keep Us Safe

1   Do you know what senses are for? Every minute of every day our senses get information and send it to our brain. We use this information to understand the world around us. With our senses we understand when food looks, smells or tastes good and fresh or when it's bad and rotten. We also feel something hot or sharp or hear when danger is coming with our senses. Our senses are very important because they keep us safe.

2   Like people, animals use their senses to find food and avoid danger. But many animals' senses are very different from people's senses.

3   For example, we use our eyes to see but bats can't see well. They have to use their ears. They make a sound and listen for an echo. They use the sound waves from the echo to 'see' how big something is and find it.

4   Snakes and lizards don't smell with their noses like us, they smell with their tongues! That's why their tongues are like a fork. The fork shape helps them understand where a smell is coming from.

5   Butterflies, on the other hand, don't taste with their tongues; they use their feet. They've got tiny taste buds there. They help the butterfly understand what flower it's standing on. That's how they know they can eat it.

6   Perhaps we see with our noses or feel with our ears. It doesn't matter. The message to our brain is the important thing. Our brain helps us understand all the messages our senses send us.

THINK BIG Why do animals use their senses differently to people? Which sense is the most important? Why?

15 Look at **14**. Read and match.

1 We use our senses
2 Bats use their ears
3 Bats use sound
4 Snakes use their tongues
5 Lizards use the shape of their tongue
6 Butterflies use their feet
7 Our brains help us

a to taste things.
b understand messages from our senses.
c to smell things.
d to see things.
e to know where a smell is coming from.
f to understand the size of something.
g to understand if something is dangerous for us.

16 Complete the chart. Which senses do you use for each of these things?

Go to a concert	Eat dinner in a restaurant	Play with a pet	Go on a roller coaster
?	?	?	?

PROJECT

17 Find out about other animal senses and make an **Animal Senses** poster. Then present it to the class.

Animal Senses

see

A chameleon can move its eyes in different directions. It uses its tongue to catch its food and taste it.

Grammar

18 Look, listen and read. Is the milkshake sweet?

Scott: I drink a milkshake at school every day. But this is my delicious new chocolate milkshake recipe. First of all, how does it smell?

Emily: Erm. It smells chocolatey.

Scott: Yes, it's got chocolate inside. Now try it. How does it taste?

Emily: It tastes cold. But yuck! It doesn't taste sweet. It tastes salty! What's in it?

Scott: Oh, no! I put salt in instead of sugar!

This	is	a milkshake.		
I	drink	it	at school	every day.
It	smells	chocolatey.		
It	doesn't taste	sweet.		

19 Complete the chart using the words from the box.

bitter hard hot rough salty soft sweet

Feel	Taste	Both
smooth	spicy	cold
sharp	sour	❓
❓	❓	
❓	❓	
❓	❓	

20 **Put the words in order. Then say.**

1 cakes My mum's delicious. taste

2 in a bakery Dad on Tuesdays. works

3 from the supermarket We flowers every day. buy

4 eating bones. doesn't like My dog

5 taste buds on their feet. Butterflies have got

6 eats two mice every week. The snake

21 **Read and choose the correct answer.**

1 When do you get up in the morning?
   a I every day get up at 6 o' clock.
   b I get up at 6 o' clock every day.
   c At 6 o' clock I get up every day.

2 Where do you eat breakfast?
   a I eat at the zoo café eggs on toast.
   b I eat eggs on toast at the zoo café.
   c At the zoo café I eat eggs on toast.

3 What's your first job?
   a The snakes' cages I clean.
   b I the snakes' cages clean.
   c I clean the snakes' cages.

4 How do they feel?
   a They're feeling smooth.
   b They are feel smooth.
   c They feel smooth.

5 Are the snakes dangerous?
   a No. The snakes friendly!
   b Snakes they are friendly.
   c No. The snakes are friendly.

6 How do they smell?
   a They smell not bad.
   b They don't smell bad.
   c They are smell bad.

22 **Play a game. Choose an object. Don't tell your partner. Ask and answer.**

Is it food?

How does it taste?

How does it feel?

Is it a lemon?

Yes.

Sour.

Rough.

Yes.

How Does Your Job Smell?

When we choose jobs, do we ever think about the smell? Read on and find out about four smelly jobs from around the world.

1 André Tyrode is from Lyon. He makes cakes and pastries every day. "Everything I make tastes and smells wonderful. It makes people want to share delicious treats together and that makes them happy. And if they're happy, I'm happy!"

Is there anything bad about his job? Well, he gets up at 5:00 a.m. every day and he usually feels very tired but the smell of fresh bread always makes him smile.

2 Alberto Rivera from Costa Rica likes his job because he can look at flowers all day. He grows and sells flowers on his farm, then sends them all over the world. "When you see all the different colours, it really helps you remember how beautiful the world is."

Do all the flowers smell good? Yes, they do but smelling that many flowers sometimes makes Alberto sneeze!

23 You've got one minute. Think of three smells that make you really happy and three smells you hate. Write them in your notebook and compare them with a partner.

118
24 Listen and read. Say whether each person's job has got a good smell or a bad smell. Then match the jobs **a–d** below to the people **1–4**.

a baker
b zookeeper
c rubbish collector
d farmer

> **CONTENT WORDS**
> clean   dreadful   fresh   look after
> smelly   stink   wet

25 Look at **24**. Which person: André, Alberto, Candace or Sarah...

1 creates something beautiful?

2 improves a place?

3 gets up early regularly?

4 sometimes gets very wet at work?

5 works with other countries?

6 has got a problem with his nose because of his job?

7 makes something people can share?

8 lives in a very clean city?

126

2 **Get ready.**

A Complete the dialogue. Use the words from the box. Then listen and check.

> awful   cold   fly
> look   swim

Morgan: Look at those penguins!

Taylor: They ¹ ? cool!

Morgan: Yeah. I like penguins. Hey, look at this: "Penguins live in the snow and ice."

Taylor: That sounds ² ? !

Morgan: Yes, very cold. Listen. "They eat fish every day." Look. They're eating fish now!

Taylor: Yuck! That looks ³ ? to me!

Morgan: Well, the penguins like it.

Taylor: Hey, look. They're swimming.

Morgan: Yes, penguins can ⁴ ? . But they can't ⁵ ? .

Taylor: Wow. I'm learning a lot about penguins!

B Practise the dialogue in **A** with a partner. Then practise again. Talk about different animals.

C Choose the words for you.

1 I **like/don't like** penguins.
2 Their food looks **delicious/terrible** to me.
3 Their home looks **warm/cold** to me.

1

2

3

4

5

6

7

8

9

3 Get set.

STEP 1 Look and read. Find out information about an animal.

STEP 2 Cut out the book outline on page 159 of your Activity Book. Fold it to make a book.

STEP 3 Write in your own animal information book. Now you're ready to **Go!**

4 Go!

A Swap books with five classmates. Write notes about their books in your notebook.

Classmate	Animal	Comment
Carla	lizards	great

B Tell the class about some of your classmates' books.

Elena's book was about sharks. Sharks are amazing!

5 **Write about yourself in your notebook.**

- What was the weather like today?
- What was the weather like yesterday?
- Today I can...
- Today I can't...

- Today the sky looks...
- My classroom feels...
- My favourite animal is...
- I like this animal because...

All About Me   Date:

How Well Do I Know It Now?

6 **Think about it. Look at page 106 and your notebook. Draw again.**

A **Use a different colour.**

B **Read and think.**

I can start the next unit.

I can ask my teacher for help and then start the next unit.

I can practise and then start the next unit.

7 **Rate this Checkpoint.**

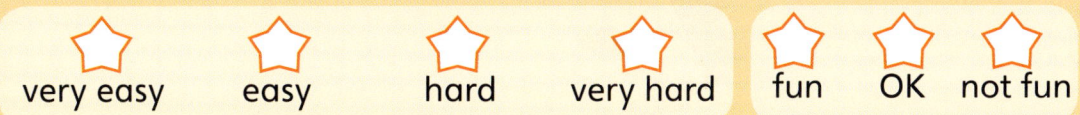

very easy   easy   hard   very hard   fun   OK   not fun

1
2
3
4
5
6
7
8
9

Units 4–6 Exam Preparation

127

Listen, colour and draw. There is one example.

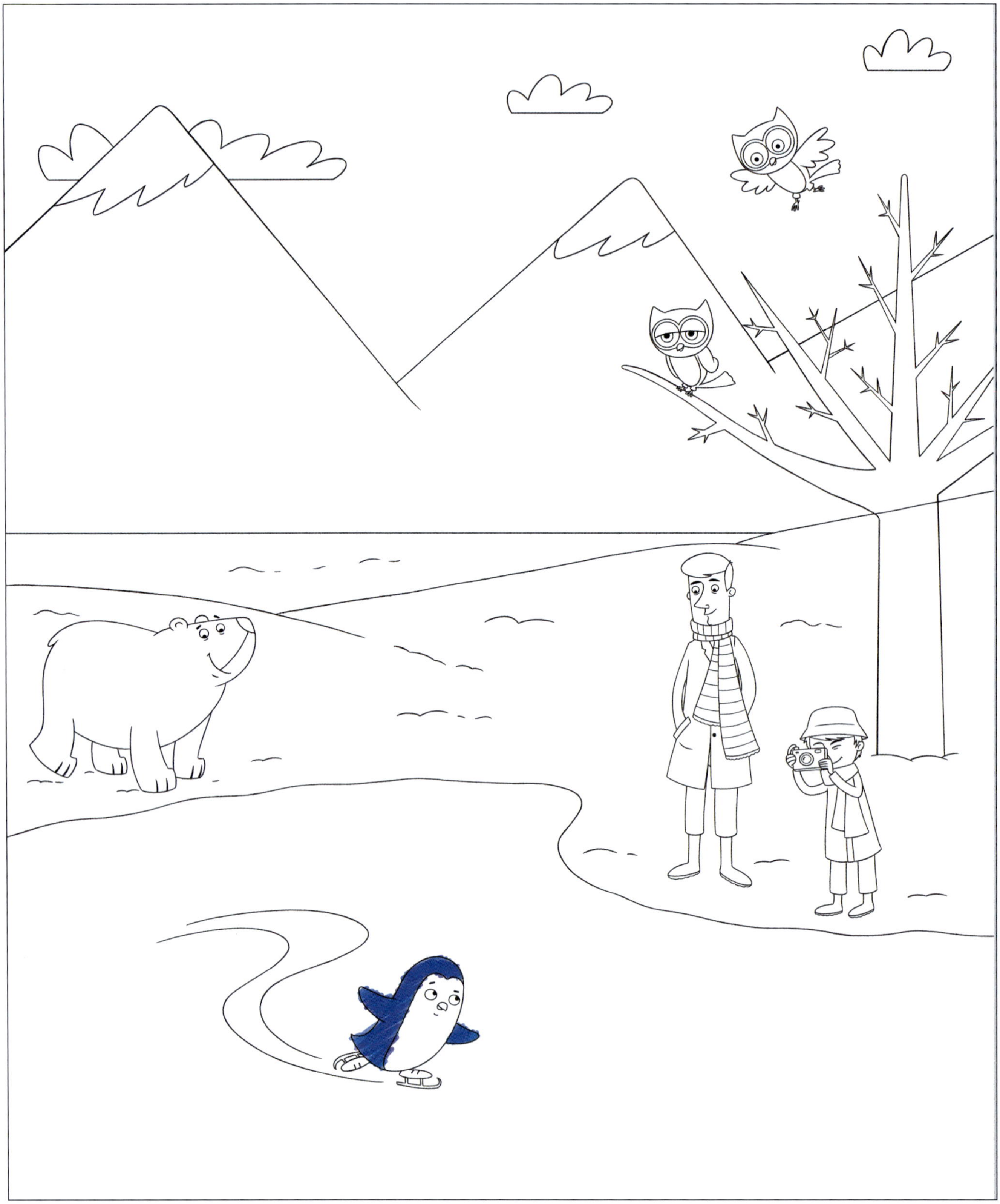

Read the text and choose the best answer. Jack is talking to his friend, Daisy.

Example

> **Jack:** What's the weather like?
> **Daisy:** A I like it when it's sunny.
>   Ⓑ It's cloudy but warm.
>   C It was hot yesterday.

Questions

1 **Jack:** Would you like to go to the lake?
  Daisy: A Yes, there's a lake.
           B Yes, you do.
           C Yes, I'd like that.

3 **Jack:** What does the ice cream taste like?
  Daisy: A Are you hungry?
           B It tastes nice!
           C The ice cream is cold.

5 **Jack:** Do we need a sweater?
  Daisy: A He needs a coat.
           B I like your sweater.
           C I think so, yes.

2 **Jack:** What can we do there?
  Daisy: A We can feed the fish.
           B We can do that.
           C We can go there.

4 **Jack:** Should we ride our bikes there?
  Daisy: A Great idea!
           B Mine is blue.
           C Yes, I can.

6 **Jack:** Is your brother coming?
  Daisy: A No, he has to study.
           B No, he wasn't here yesterday.
           C No, he works in a store.

Fabulous Food!

128

1 Listen, look and say.

At *Your Way Café* you decide what to put in your sandwich or on your pizza. There are so many things to choose from. Which will you choose?

1 Super Sandwiches!

1 bread

2 cucumbers

3 turkey

4 mustard

5 lettuce

2 Pizza Perfection!

6 green peppers

7 mushrooms

8 tomato sauce

9 olives

10 onions

129

2 Listen, find and say.

3 Play a game.

4 Listen and sing. What do they eat?

I'm Hungry!

Hi, Mum, I'm home from school.
I'm really hungry now.
I'd like to make a sandwich,
Can you show me how?

I am home from my school day.
I'd like a sandwich. Is that OK?

Are there any olives?
Here are some on the shelf.
Is there any tomato sauce?
I see it for myself.

Chorus

There's just one problem, Mum
There isn't any bread!
But I've got a great idea:
Let's have pizza instead!

Chorus

5 Look at **1**. Ask and answer.

What do you like in your sandwiches?

I like turkey and lettuce.

 **THINK BIG** What is good on pizzas and in sandwiches?

133

6 Listen and read. What are Luke and Amy making?

A Surprise for Mum

Are there any tomatoes for the pizza?

I can't see any but there's some cheese.

1 Luke and Amy are making dinner for their mum. It's a surprise.

Are there any onions?

No, there aren't. But there's a green pepper.

2 They need toppings for their pizza.

This cheese is yummy.

Mmm. These olives taste delicious, too!

3 Amy and Luke taste some of the pizza toppings.

Oh, no! There isn't any more cheese.

And there aren't any more olives. Oops.

4 They look in the fridge again. What can they use?

5 | Amy and Luke look for more food.

6 | There's a surprise for Mum in the kitchen but it isn't dinner.

 Read and say true or false.

1 Amy and Luke want to make breakfast for their mother.
2 There aren't any onions for the pizza.
3 Amy and Luke eat all the cheese and olives.
4 There isn't any turkey.
5 There isn't a surprise for Mum.

THINK BIG What do you think Amy and Luke's mum does next? Why? How can they help their mum?

8 Listen and look at the sentences. Help Luke and Amy make more.

turkey | tomatoes | bread | mushrooms

There's some | cheese | .

There isn't any | cheese | .

Is there any | cheese | ?

There are some | olives | .

There aren't any | olives | .

Are there any | olives | ?

9 Read and choose.

1 There's **some/any** tomato sauce on the pizza.

2 There are **some/any** sandwiches in my bag.

3 There aren't **some/any** olives in the kitchen.

4 There isn't **some/any** lettuce in my sandwich.

5 Are there **any/some** olives? Yes, there are.

6 **Is/Are** there any cheese? Yes, there is.

10 Make the questions.

1 No, there isn't. There isn't any bread.

2 Yes, there are some bananas. I think there are four.

3 Yes, there is. The lettuce is in the fridge.

4 No, there aren't any mushrooms in the soup. Don't worry!

5 Yes, there are some strawberries. They're next to the mangoes.

136

11 **Complete the dialogue in pairs. Then listen and check.**

Rob: Mum, can we have pizza for dinner?

Mum: Good idea. Look in the fridge. Is there ¹ 🔑 tomato sauce?

Rob: Yes, there ² 🔑 .

Mum: Is ³ 🔑 any cheese?

Rob: Yes, there is. There are ⁴ 🔑 mushrooms and some onions.

Mum: Great! What about olives? ⁵ 🔑 there ⁶ 🔑 olives?

Rob: No, there ⁷ 🔑 .

Mum: That's OK, Dad doesn't like olives. We can have pizza for dinner.

Rob: Brilliant. Let's start now.

12 **Look and make sentences in pairs. There is the food in blue and there isn't the food in red.**

bananas   bread   cheese   cucumbers   lettuce   mushrooms

There's…

… some cheese.

13 **Look. Ask and answer about the sandwich.**

Is there any turkey for your sandwich?

Yes, there is.

Are there any mushrooms for your sandwich?

No, there aren't.

language practice (*Is there any…?/Are there any…?*) Unit 7 **117**

14 Work with a partner. Guess if these statements are **true** or **false**.

1 You can only find vitamins in fruit and vegetables.

2 There aren't any vitamins in chocolate.

3 There's lots of vitamin A in orange fruits and vegetables.

4 The human body can make vitamin D.

5 All vitamins live inside our bodies for years.

15 137 Listen and read. How many different fruits and vegetables should we eat each day? Then check your answers in **14**.

> **CONTENT WORDS**
>
> blood   bone   brain   energy   fat/water soluble
> healthy   iron   muscle   skin   teeth   vitamin

The Vitamin Alphabet

Vitamins help our bodies grow strong and stay healthy. We need vitamins every day and we have to get them from the food we eat. There are two types of vitamins. Some of them live in the fat in our body and stay in our bodies. Others live in the water in our bodies. They don't stay around for long. But which foods do we get our vitamins from? And why do we need them?

Let's start with the fat soluble vitamins: A, D and E.

Vitamin A: There's lots of Vitamin A in orange and yellow fruits like carrots or mangoes but you can also find some in milk and the yellow part of eggs. Vitamin A helps your eyes and skin stay healthy.

Vitamin D: Milk and eggs have also got vitamin D in them and so does fish. When we sit in the sun, our body makes a lot of it naturally. This vitamin is very important for strong bones.

Vitamin E: This, on the other hand, helps keep our blood healthy. You can get vitamin E when you eat nuts and green vegetables.

The water soluble vitamins, B and C are just as important.

Vitamin C: Vitamin C is good for our bones, teeth and even our brains. We get this vitamin from oranges, peppers, tomatoes and potatoes. Vitamin C also helps us keep other important substances in our body. Iron for example.

Vitamin B: There are many different kinds of Vitamin B. Some help give us energy to move our muscles. Others help make blood. We get the different kinds of Vitamin B from different kinds of food. These include potatoes, bananas, bread, rice, pasta, chicken, fish, cheese, eggs and green peppers.

We should eat a good variety of fruit and vegetables – at least five a day – and lots of other healthy foods like brown bread, milk, eggs and fish. That way, we always get the vitamins we need. But we can eat some 'naughty' things, too. For example, there are three B vitamins in a good bar of dark chocolate!

THINK BIG Which vitamins do the following people need and why?
a a football player   **b** a pilot

16 **Look at 15. Read and answer the questions. Write the answers in your notebook.**

1 What are the two types of vitamins?

2 How are they different?

3 Is it more important to eat one group every day? Why?

4 Why is it good to get lots of Vitamin A?

5 Which foods contain Vitamin E?

6 Which vitamin has lots of different ones?

7 Which vitamin do we get from the sun?

17 **Where do you get your vitamins from? Complete the chart. Tell your partner.**

	Food	Vitamins
Breakfast		
Snack		
Lunch		
Dinner		

PROJECT

18 **Imagine you're teaching other children about vitamins and where you find them. Make a Vitamin Plate and present it to the class. Make sure you include all the vitamins and different food groups.**

There are carrots on my plate because there's a lot of Vitamin A in carrots. Vitamin A is good for our skin.

Grammar

19 Look, listen and read. Does Dan have a healthy dinner?

Jenna: Is that your dinner? There's a lot of meat and a lot of bread but there isn't much fruit and there aren't many vegetables!

Dan: There are some vegetables with my meal. Look, there's an onion and I've got a few potatoes. There's also a little lettuce and tomato ketchup in my burger. How many vegetables do I have to eat?

Jenna: Well, there aren't many vitamins in those! Look! You have to eat a lot of fruit and vegetables to get your vitamins!

Dan: That's OK. You've got a big salad and some fruit. You can eat the vitamins for me!

You've got **a** big salad. I've got **an** onion. You've got **some** fruit. There's **a lot of** meat. There's **a little** tomato ketchup.	There are **some** vegetables with my meal. You have to eat **a lot of** vegetables. I've got **a few** potatoes.
There isn't **much** fruit.	There aren't **many** vegetables.
How much fruit do I have to eat?	**How many** vegetables do I have to eat?

20 Read and choose.

1 There's **an/a** orange in my bag.

2 There isn't **some/much** cheese on this pizza!

3 I don't like **many/much** pizza toppings.

4 Can I have **a/some** glass of milk?

5 Mum makes **a lot of/a few** food for birthday parties.

6 There are only **a few/a little** vitamins in chocolate.

7 I don't eat **some/much** bread for breakfast.

8 Please put **a few/some** sugar on my cereal.

21 Complete the statements with **much**, **many**, **a little** or **a few**.

1 I don't eat ? chips. They aren't good for you.

2 I eat ? chocolate every day – it's healthy.

3 There aren't ? vitamins in popcorn.

4 Dad drinks ? cups of coffee a day. Is that bad?

5 I don't eat ? cheese. There's a lot of fat in it.

6 Mum says I can't have ? ketchup on my burger. Why not?

22 Complete the quiz questions. Use **How much** or **How many**.

1 ? meat do you eat?
2 ? times a week do you eat fish?
3 ? fruit and vegetables do you eat every day?
4 ? healthy snacks do you eat?
5 ? fizzy drinks or sweets do you have each day?
6 ? exercise do you do?

23 Complete Keira's answer to the quiz questions.

> a few (x2)   little   lot of (x2)   many   much (x2)   some

I don't eat ¹? meat because I don't really like it. I eat fish though. I think fish is delicious. Every day, I eat ²? fruit and I eat a ³? vegetables, too because I don't like meat. I eat one small snack in the morning, usually ⁴? nuts or sometimes a ⁵? yoghurt. I know I sound like a goody goody but I really don't eat ⁶? chocolate. Not ⁷? teenagers can say that! And I only drink ⁸? fizzy drinks because I only drink them at parties. And of course I do a ⁹? exercise. I'm on the swim team!

24 Now ask and answer the quiz questions in **22** with a partner. Then write about your answers in your notebook.

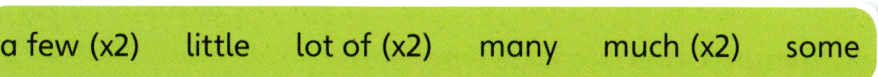

I eat a little meat. I like eating some chicken or a burger once or twice a week.

Breakfast in Different Countries
What do YOU get?

Katie, UK

Today I'm writing about breakfast. My mum says breakfast is the most important meal of the day so she puts a healthy breakfast on the table every day at 7:30 a.m. On school days, we eat cereal with milk and a banana, boiled eggs and brown bread soldiers or just toast with marmite. On Saturdays or Sundays, we usually have bacon and tomato butties with a few strawberries or blueberries on the side. That tastes great! But this Saturday morning, breakfast was awful! It was porridge – yuck. That's oat cereal with hot milk. Mum loves it and she eats it every day with some honey. But why do we have to eat it? And on a Saturday, too! What do you all eat for breakfast?

Yoko, Japan

That sounds OK! My family never eats any cereal. In the morning, I usually eat rice, soup, fish and pickles.

25 **Discuss with a partner.**

1 Do you eat breakfast every day?
2 What time do you usually eat it?
3 What are some of the things that people eat for breakfast in your country?
4 What's your favourite breakfast at weekends?

26 **Listen and read Katie's blog. What does she say about her breakfast today?**

> **CONTENT WORDS**
> blueberries   boiled/fried eggs   cereal
> doughnut   honey   oats   porridge   toast

27 **Look at 26. Answer the questions in 25 for Katie.**

28 **Look and match the breakfasts to the correct country.**

1 U.K.   2 Japan   3 Mexico   4 Australia   5 Spain

a    b    c    d    e

Luis, Spain

I like fish but I never eat it for breakfast! I usually eat bread or cereal for breakfast, too but sometimes at weekends I eat churros with chocolate. Churros are like little doughnuts. They're delicious!

Camilla, Mexico

We often eat eggs for breakfast but they aren't boiled. They're fried. They're called huevos rancheros. We put them on toasted tortillas with some salsa. They are spicy, colourful and delicious! What's marmite?

Tony, Australia

Marmite is brown and salty and you can put it on your toast. We eat it here, too but it's called Vegemite :-). We sometimes eat porridge, too, I think it's OK. I put cream and a little brown sugar on top. But I really like eating toast in the morning – with beans on top! Yum! Do you eat that in the U.K.?

Katie, UK

Thanks for writing everybody. Huevos rancheros and churros with chocolate sound yummy!

29 **Think about these questions. Then compare with a partner.**

1 Which breakfast do you like? Why?
2 Which breakfast don't you like? Why?
3 Which breakfast is healthy?
4 Which breakfast isn't healthy?

30 **Find out about breakfasts in three other countries. Share with the class.**

In Turkey, people eat cheese, olives and salad for breakfast.

THINK BIG Why is it important to eat a good breakfast? Where do people eat these for breakfast? Find out!

a kippers   b kimchi   c potato pancakes

142

31 **Listen and read. Then match.**

Title – says what you are writing about
Topic sentence – explains the main idea
Detail sentences – add more information
Final sentence – summarises and gives an opinion

detail sentences   final sentence   title   topic sentence

1 **My Favourite Breakfast**
by Laura Brown

2 I like a lot of different things for breakfast but I have my favourite breakfast every Sunday morning.

3 I start with some orange slices, cold from the fridge. Then my mother makes two fluffy pancakes for me. I put butter on them and then I put warm maple syrup on top. The pancakes are delicious with a glass of cold milk.

4 My favourite breakfast makes Sundays special.

Writing Steps

32 **Write about your favourite breakfast.**

1 Think about your favourite breakfast.
2 Write a title.
3 Write a topic sentence.
4 Add details to give more information.
5 Write a final sentence.

143

33 **Listen, read and repeat.**

1 br **2** cr **3** dr **4** fr **5** gr **6** pr **7** tr

144

34 **Listen and find. Then say.**

bread   **cr**eam   **dr**eam   **fr**og

grass   **pr**ize   **tr**ain

145

35 **Listen and blend the sounds.**

1 d-r-i-ve   drive   **2** g-r-ee-n   green
3 b-r-ow-n   brown   **4** p-r-i-n-ce prince
5 c-r-y   cry   **6** t-r-o-ll   troll
7 f-r-o-m   from   **8** b-r-i-ck   brick

146

36 **Read aloud. Then listen and chant.**

Every night,
I dream
About a prince
And a troll
And a green frog!
In my dream,
They eat bread
With cream.

148

37 Listen. Look at the poster. Which dish looks good to you? Discuss with a partner.

Peruvians love potatoes. Peru grows more than 2,300 types of potatoes. There are many different shapes, sizes and colours!

Potatoes grow very well in the cool weather, high in the Andes Mountains.

Potatoes in Peru

The most famous dish is *papa a la huancaína* – potatoes in a spicy cheese sauce.

Another is *papa rellena*, or stuffed potato. This dish has meat, onions and eggs stuffed inside a potato.

I want to try the stuffed potato. It looks delicious!

PROJECT

38 Make a poster about the food in a country other than your own.

1 Learn about the typical foods in that country.

2 Cut out pictures of the foods.

3 Label the pictures.

4 Share your poster with the class.

CHINA

noodles

dumplings

fried rice

39 **Read and match.**

1 I've got a

2 They eat a lot of

3 I don't like many salads.

4 How much salt is in this?

5 How many slices do you want?

a Only a few seem tasty to me.

b big pizza.

c I've put only a little.

d Three, please.

e oranges.

40 **Read and choose. Then role play.**

Juanita: Hi, Mum. I'm really hungry. Can I have a snack, please?

Mum: Have some fruit.

Juanita: **Is/Are** there any strawberries?

Mum: I don't think so.

Juanita: Is there **any/some** pineapple?

Mum: No, there isn't. What about an apple?

Juanita: Is there any **cheese/olives**?

Mum: Yes, there **is/isn't**.

Juanita: Great. A cheese sandwich!

Mum: Sorry, but there **isn't/aren't** any bread.

Juanita: Well, I think I'll have an apple then.

41 **Make a pizza. Ask and answer to find two people with the same pizza. Use the words from the box.**

cheese   chicken   cucumbers   mushrooms   olives
onion   peppers   tomato sauce   turkey

Is there any cheese on your pizza?

Yes, there is.

I Can

● ask and answer about food.

● talk about vitamins and how they help my body.

● find different parts of a paragraph.

Healthy Living

1 Listen, look and say.

149

> How do you feel today? Find out how healthy Sally and Zach are, then ask yourself!

I feel great today.

1 Did she... have a big breakfast?

5 Did he... eat breakfast?

2 Did she... get 10 hours sleep last night?

6 Did he... get any exercise?

3 Did she... drink lots of water?

7 Did he... have a healthy lunch?

4 Did she... ride her bike?

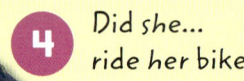

8 Did he... get enough sleep?

2 Listen, find and say.   150

3 Play a game.

128 Unit 8 vocabulary (healthy and unhealthy activities)

4 Listen and sing. How does Zach feel today?

Live Right!

Did you eat breakfast? asks Mum,
You don't look good to me.
Did you get enough sleep? asks Mum,
Did you watch too much TV?

**Enough sleep. Good food.
Be healthy. Live right!
Enough sleep. Good food.
Be healthy. Live right!**

Did you ride your bike? asks Mum,
You know it's good for you.
Did you get any exercise?
You know it's good to do!

Chorus

I feel awful today.

5 Look at **1**. Ask and answer.

Did he eat breakfast?

Did she ride her bike?

No, he didn't.

Yes, she did.

THINK BIG Which child in **1** are you like? Explain why.

Story

6 **Listen and read. Did Amy eat a healthy dinner?**

1   Amy's dad wants her to be healthy.

2   Amy likes unhealthy food.

3   Amy likes chips but fried food isn't very healthy.

4   Amy likes cola.

5 Amy knows her dinner wasn't really healthy. She didn't eat many vegetables.

6 Now Amy doesn't feel well. She needs to eat healthy food.

7 Read and choose.

1 Amy had dinner at a **party/home**.
2 Amy likes **healthy/unhealthy** food.
3 Chips are fried **potatoes/onions**.
4 Fried food is **good/bad** for you.
5 Cola has got a lot of **fruit/sugar** in it.
6 Amy's dad **is/isn't** happy about Amy's dinner.

THINK BIG What should Amy eat for her next dinner? Why?

Language in Action

155

8 **Listen and look at the sentences. Help Luke and Amy make more.**

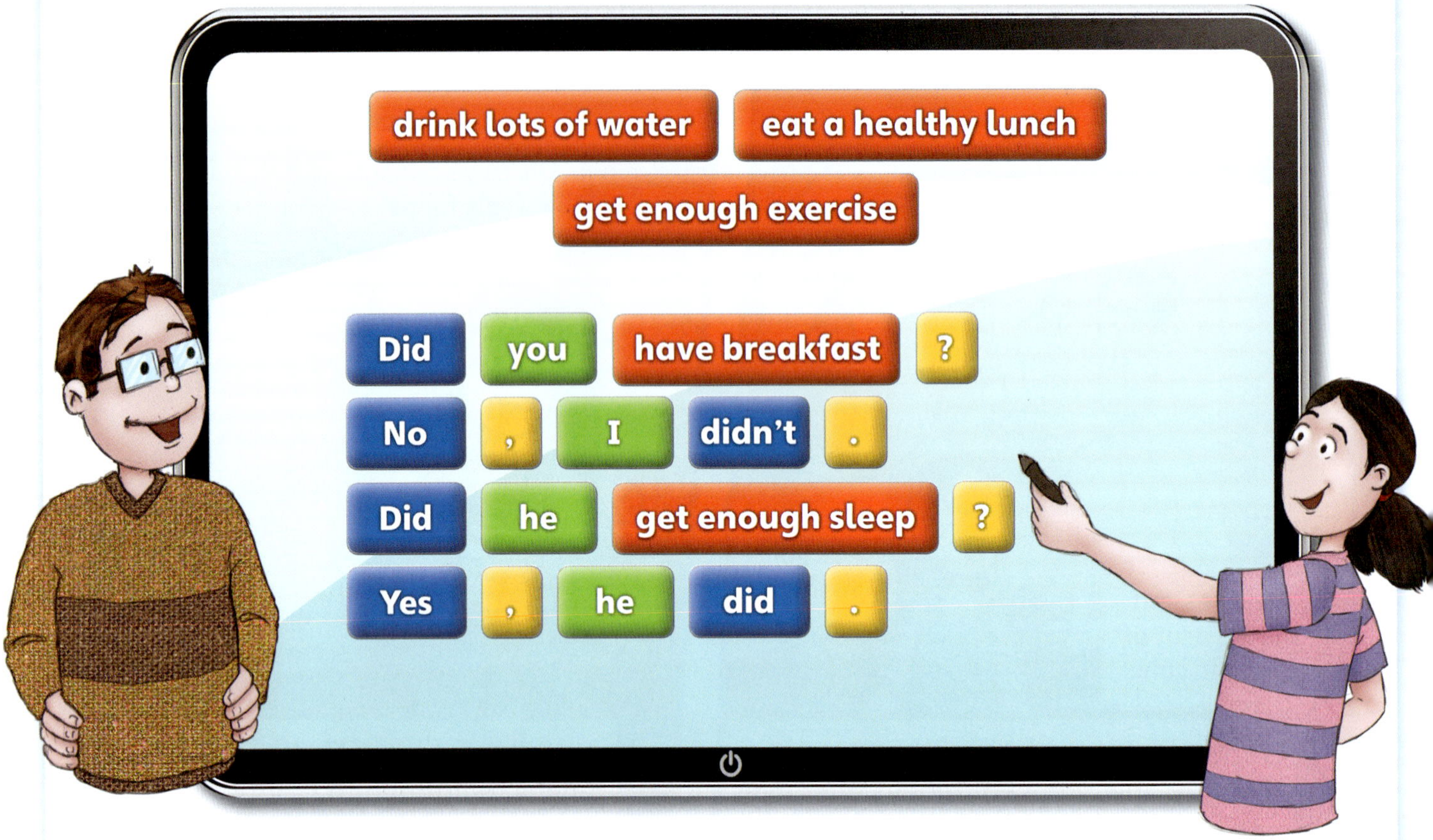
drink lots of water
eat a healthy lunch
get enough exercise
Did you have breakfast ?
No , I didn't .
Did he get enough sleep ?
Yes , he did .

9 **Match the phrases. Make five questions about yesterday. Then ask and answer.**

1 do any	**a** of water
2 drink lots	**b** healthy lunch
3 have a	**c** sleep
4 get enough	**d** my bike
5 ride	**e** exercise

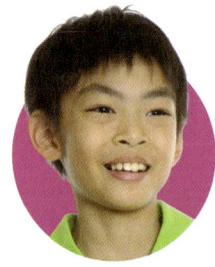

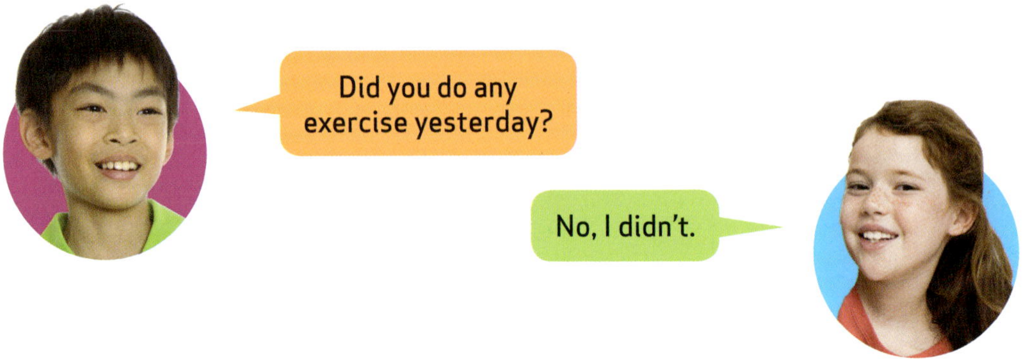
Did you do any exercise yesterday?
No, I didn't.

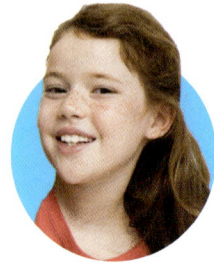

10 **Complete the dialogues. Use did or didn't.**

1 **A:** Good morning, Katia. ❓ you eat breakfast?

   B: Yes, I ❓ .

2 **A:** ❓ Ted take a shower this morning?

   B: No, he ❓ .

3 **A:** ❓ the football team get enough sleep before the game?

   B: No, they ❓ .

4 **A:** ❓ Melissa brush her teeth?

   B: Yes, she ❓ .

11 **Put the words in order to make questions. Then ask.**

1 yesterday? | Did | get | enough | Alice | sleep

2 play football | last week? | Did | after school | they

3 a shower | Did | have | this morning? | you

4 play | video games | weekend? | we | Did | at the

5 on Sunday? | go | Matthew | Did | to the park

12 **Read and match. Now change the answers.**

1 Did Ruth visit her cousin yesterday?

2 Did you go to a national park?

3 Did Mike like the band?

4 Did your mum and dad watch a DVD?

5 Did Melanie have onions on her pizza?

6 Did you learn a lot at school today?

a Yes, they did. It was great.

b Yes, I did. I learned about healthy and unhealthy food.

c No, she didn't. She hates them!

d Yes, she did. She was glad to see her.

e No, he didn't. He doesn't like going to concerts.

f No, we didn't. It was too cold and snowy.

13 **Read, guess and choose.**

1 How much exercise is good for children?

    a 60 minutes or more every day

    b 30 minutes three times a week

2 Which activity uses more energy?

    a playing computer games

    b playing football

14 157 **Listen and read. What are the numbers 60, 12,000, 9 and 10? Then check your answers in 13.**

What Is a Calorie?

> **CONTENT WORDS**
> active   activities   body   burn   calorie
> fit   measure   put on weight   rest

www.teen_health.org

Exercise, eating and sleeping are important parts of our daily routine. Exercise every day for at least 60 minutes. Eat the correct number of calories so that you have the energy to exercise. Get the correct amount of rest. Read on to answer some simple questions.

What are calories? Are they important?

A calorie is a measure of the energy you get from food. Some foods are high in calories and other foods aren't. Your body needs a certain number of calories to do all the things you do every day. But if you eat more calories than your body needs, you put on too much weight. Lots of activity and exercise burns a lot of calories. Very little activity or exercise doesn't burn a lot of calories. For example, Michael Phelps, the Olympic Swimmer, ate 12,000 calories every day during the Olympic Games but he didn't put on weight because he burnt all the calories!

Why is being active good for us?

It helps our hearts stay healthy. It makes our bones strong and it creates muscles. Being active is really important for young and old people. Activities that use lots of energy are best. Dancing is really good for your body. Riding a bike and swimming are also good for your body. But watching TV or playing video games are bad for your health if you do them too much. That's because you sit in the same place to do them.

Is there a right amount of sleep?

Yes. Sleeping is good for your health but sleeping too much or too little is definitely bad for you. Doctors say between 9 and 10 hours of sleep is best for teenagers. When we sleep, we rest our bodies and our brains. Then we're ready for activity again the next day.

Paying attention to what exercise you do helps you stay fit. How much do you do? How much time do you spend in front of the TV or computer? How many hours a night do you sleep? Do you eat the right things? Be honest!

THINK BIG How do you feel when you sleep too little or too much? Why is it bad for you?

15 Look at **14**. Answer the questions in your notebook.

1 What's a calorie?

2 Why do people put on weight?

3 Why didn't Michael Phelps put on weight?

4 What does exercise or activity do for our bodies?

5 Why is watching TV or playing video games unhealthy?

16 Complete the chart. Use the activities from the box. Then add more activities.

> dancing   playing a sport   playing video games   riding my bike to school
> sleeping for 13 hours   watching TV

Good for your body	Bad for your body

17 Work with a partner. Ask and answer the questions at the end of the article in **14**.

How much exercise do you do?

PROJECT

18 Make an **Exercise Chart** for you. Show good activities and bad activities. Are you fit and healthy?

Day of the week	Activity	Number of hours	Good or bad
On Monday	Dancing	2 hours	Good – dancing is good for you. It keeps you fit and burns calories.

I ride my bike to school every day and I swim twice a week. I play basketball every Saturday, too.

19 159 Look, listen and read. How did Donna's dad come home?

Donna: In 2005, my dad was a champion cyclist but he stopped in 2007 because he hurt his knee. Last week, the doctor said his knee was better. Yesterday, Dad started a new healthy living programme. He went to bed early and he slept for eight hours. When he got up, he ate a good healthy breakfast, he made a healthy lunch, he put it in his backpack and he rode his bicycle to work. He cycled ten kilometres to work and then he cycled another ten kilometres home.

Brad: Wow! I saw a man with a fantastic bicycle an hour ago. He looked really fit. Was that your dad?

Donna: No. Dad came home two hours ago. When he arrived, he sat on the sofa and he fell asleep straight away!

		play**ed**.
	I/You/He/She/It/We/They	walk**ed**.
		stay**ed**.
	start – **ed**	start**ed**
	tid**y** – **ied**	tid**ied**
	lik**e** – **d**	lik**ed**
	st**op** – **ped**	stop**ped**
But...	I/You/He/She/It/We/They	**went**.
		saw.
		came.

20 Copy the chart in your notebook and complete. Use the words from the box.

> bake carry change climb cry drop exercise
> finish help join love tip try worry

start**ed**	tid**ied**	lik**ed**	stop**ped**
?	?	?	?

21 **Read and complete.**

1

> Ffyona Campbell's dad ❓ (work) for the Royal Navy. When she was a little girl, she ❓ (move) house 24 times and ❓ (live) in a lot of different countries. When Ffyona was 21, she ❓ (travel) across Australia on foot. She ❓ (walk) 80 kilometres a day for 95 days and ❓ (complete) 54,000 kilometres from Sydney to Perth.

2

> In November 2012, Okan Kaya from Australia ❓ (play) the longest video game marathon. It ❓ (last) 135 hours, 15 minutes and 10 seconds. He only ❓ (stop) the game after seven days.

22 **Read and match.**

1	go	a	wrote
2	come	b	slept
3	have	c	put
4	sleep	d	went
5	fall	e	had
6	write	f	came
7	fly	g	flew
8	put	h	fell

23 **Tell your partner about what you did yesterday.**

Yesterday, I woke up early and walked to school.

Yesterday, I went to the park after school. I played football.

Strange Sports

Almost everyone knows about football, baseball and basketball. But do you know anything about Octopush, Footvolley or Pumpkin Regattas? Read about these strange sports and how they began!

Octopush

Octopush comes from England but people now play it all over the world. A scuba diving club invented the game in 1954. During the winter, it was very cold to do scuba diving in the sea so they played Octopush in their swimming pool. It's a bit like hockey but people play it under water. Players use a small stick. They try to push a puck or 'squid' into a net to score points for their team. They called the game 'octo' – push because there were eight players. Unfortunately it isn't much fun to watch because you can't see the players!

24 **Work with a partner. In which countries do you think these sports are popular? Match the sports to different countries. Choose from these or add your own.**

Australia

France

New Zealand

1 baseball   2 cricket
3 football   4 rugby
5 ice hockey   6 cycling

United States of America

Canada

United Kingdom

160
25 **Listen and read. When did people start these strange sports?**

> **CONTENT WORDS**
> contest   court   net   puck   race   regatta   rowing   scuba diving   team

26 **Look at 25. Read and say true or false.**

1 You play Octopush in the sea.
2 You can't see the players in an Octopush match.
3 In Brazil, in 1965, people played football on the beach.
4 In Footvolley, you can't use your hands.
5 There's only one Pumpkin Regatta each year.

Footvolley

Footvolley is a sport from Brazil. The game started on Copacabana beach in 1965. Football players weren't allowed to play football on the beach then. When the police came, they went to the beach volleyball courts and played there. They invented Footvolley. It's just like volleyball but the players use a football. Players have to pass the ball to the other team over a high net. They can't touch the ball with their hands. People still play Footvolley on the beach today. It's very exciting but very difficult! Many famous Brazilian football players also play Footvolley.

Pumpkin Regatta

In the autumn, in parts of the United States and Canada, people join in a contest called a Pumpkin Regatta. It's like a boat race but the players don't race in boats. They race in giant, hollowed out pumpkins! The pumpkin races started in 1999 in Windsor in Nova Scotia. A man there grew giant pumpkins and he decided to use them for rowing. Soon other places wanted to have their own regattas and pumpkin racing became very popular. The pumpkins weigh more than 450 kilos. After the race, there's usually a pumpkin pie-eating contest.

27 **Complete this chart about the sports.**

	Octopush	Footvolley	Pumpkin Regatta
Where is it from?			
What is it?			
What sport(s) is it like?			
Why did it start?			

THINK BIG Why did these sports start in these places? Can you do these sports in other countries?

162

28 Complete these sentences. Then listen and check.

> I go to bed at 9:00 and wake up at 7:00.
> Dad eats cheese but Mum doesn't eat cheese.
> We can go to the park or go to the cinema.

and   but   or

1 I like eating olives ❓ I don't like eating tomatoes.
2 I never clean my room ❓ take out the rubbish.
3 I get dressed at 7:15 ❓ I go to school at 8:30.

29 Join these sentences. Then write.

1 My sister plays tennis. My brother plays baseball. (*and*)
2 I usually eat eggs in the morning. This morning, I'm having pancakes. (*but*)
3 We can have chicken for dinner. We can try the new restaurant. (*or*)
4 There aren't any onions in the fridge. There are some green peppers. (*but*)
5 My dad works at a hospital. My mum works at a school. (*and*)

30 Read and choose.

I don't like playing sports **¹but/or** I need to get some exercise. I usually play video games after school **²but/or** I watch a DVD. My sister likes playing tennis **³and/but** volleyball but I don't. But I love going hiking with my family in the mountains. It's cool to see lots of animals **⁴and/but** birds.

31 Write three sentences about healthy habits. Use **and**, **but** and **or** once.

163

32 Listen, read and repeat.

1 all   **2** au   **3** aw

 164

33 Listen and find. Then say.

b**all**   h**au**l   dr**aw**

 165

34 Listen and blend the sounds.

1 s-m-all   small   **2** c-all   call
3 t-all   tall   **4** y–aw-n   yawn
5 c-l-aw   claw   **6** w-all   wall
7 l-aw   law   **8** P-aul   Paul

 **166**

35 Read aloud. Then listen and chant.

I'm Paul, I'm bored.
Yawn, yawn.
Let's play, let's play
With a ball,
Let's draw, let's draw
A wall.

36 **Look and listen. Point to and say the healthy activities.**

a    b    c    d

37 **Work with a partner. Tell your partner to do healthy things.**

Don't watch TV. Go outside and play with a ball!

Ride your bike at a park or in your neighborhood. It's fun and it's good for you.

PROJECT

38 **Work with a group. Think of a new game you can play outside. Write down the rules. Teach the rest of the class your new game.**

39 **Read and choose. Then say.**

1 Did she **eat/eating** a fruit salad at lunchtime?

2 **Did/Don't** you do any exercise yesterday?

3 Did they drink lots of water today? No, they **did/didn't**.

4 Lenny is tired. He **didn't/don't** get enough sleep last night.

40 **Do a survey of your classmates. Add two of your own questions. Ask and answer.**

1 eat/healthy/food?

2 get/sleep/last night?

3 do/exercise/last week?

4 brush/teeth/this morning?

5 ride/bike/at the weekend?

6 drink/lots/water/today?

7 ❓

8 ❓

 Did you get enough sleep last night?

Yes, I did.

41 **Read and complete.**

1 Mehmet ❓ (sleep) for twelve hours last night.

2 The cat ❓ (stop) drinking milk.

3 Mum and Dad ❓ (go) to the mountains at the weekend.

4 My friend ❓ (fall) out of a tree in the park yesterday.

5 I ❓ (join) the swimming club today.

6 Anita ❓ (carry) my bag to school for me.

I Can

• talk about healthy and unhealthy habits.

• ask and answer about activities in the past.

• use *and*, *or* and *but* in sentences.

Unit 9 — School Trips!

169
1 Listen, look and say.

Top **8** places to visit!

1 museum

2 dairy farm

3 art gallery

4 national park

5 theatre

6 zoo

7 concert hall

8 aquarium

170
2 Listen, find and say.

3 Play a game.

4 Listen and sing. Did she visit the zoo?

Learning Out of School

I like going on school trips,
Learning out of school.
We go to lots of places.
They're interesting and cool!

Aquarium, theatre, concert hall and zoo,
We saw some great things.
There was lots to do!

**School trips. School trips.
They're a lot of fun.
School trips. School trips.
Let's go on one!**

Where did you go?
What did you see?
We went to the zoo, we saw a play,
We had a great time!

Chorus

Zoo
ADMIT ONE

5 Look at 1. Ask and answer.

It was a
sunny day.

Yes, I did.

Did you go to a
national park?

THINK BIG **Why is it good to go on school trips?**

Story

6 Listen and read. Did Luke enjoy the trip?

A Cool Trip

1 Amy and Luke went on a trip today.

2 They went to a big park where there are very old rocks.

3 Their guide told them a lot of things about the rocks in the park.

4 Amy liked the park.

5 Luke didn't like the trip. He didn't like walking a lot.

6 Luke doesn't want to see another rock!

7 **Read and answer.**

1 Where did Luke and Amy go on their trip?

2 What did they learn about?

3 Did Amy like the trip? Why/Why not?

4 Did Luke enjoy the trip? Why/Why not?

5 What did Amy get for Luke in the gift shop?

THINK BIG **What national parks are there in your country? Why have we got national parks?**

Language in Action

175

8 **Listen and look at the sentences. Help Luke and Amy make more.**

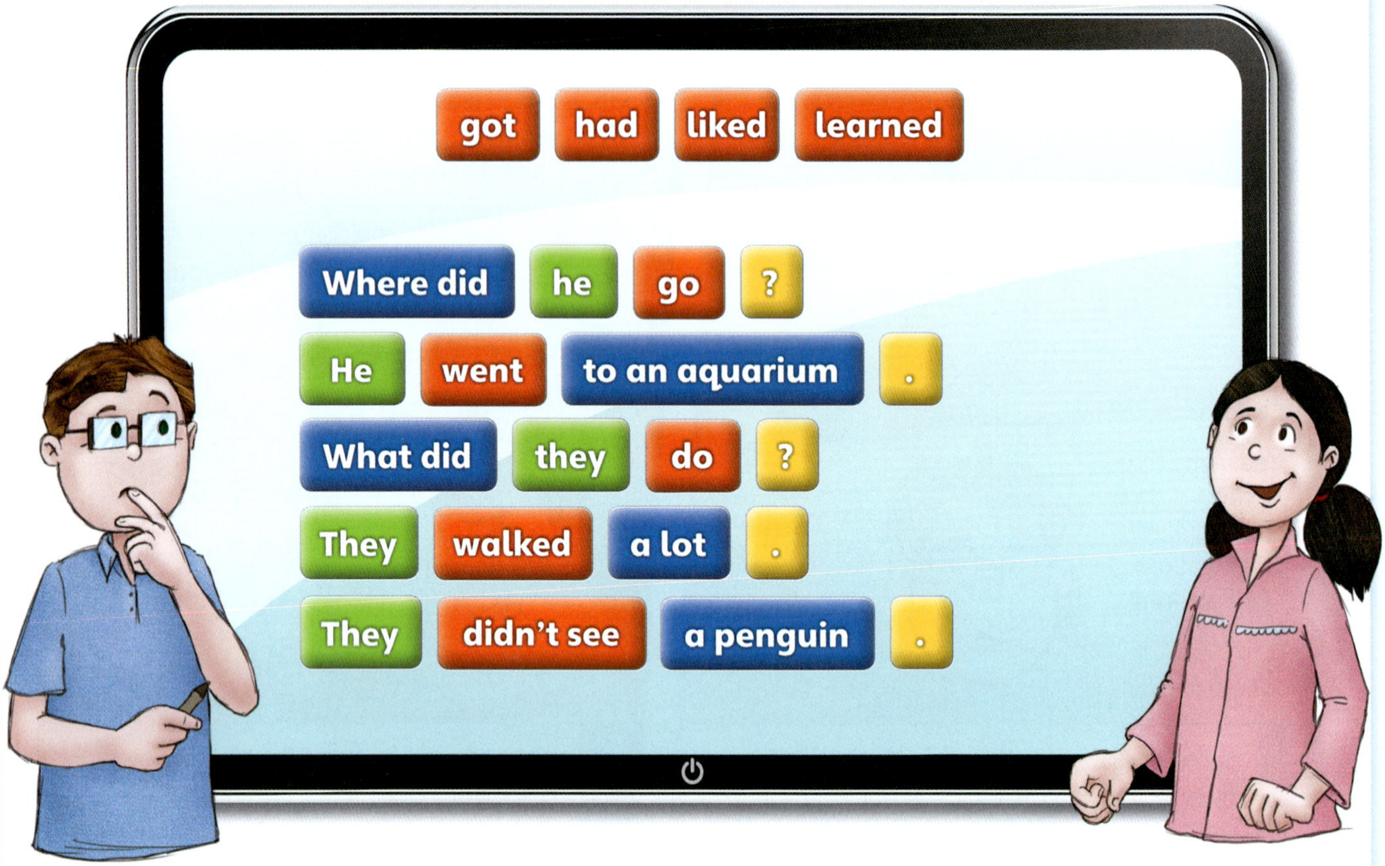
got had liked learned
Where did he go ?
He went to an aquarium .
What did they do ?
They walked a lot .
They didn't see a penguin .

9 **Complete the chart. Then make new sentences.**

did (x2)   didn't   go   saw   went

1	Where	did	they	?	?	They	went	to the zoo.
2	What	?	she	do	?	She	?	a play.
3		Did	you	like it	?	Yes, I	?	
4		Did	you	go to the museum	?	No, I	? go	to the museum.

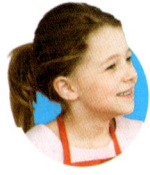

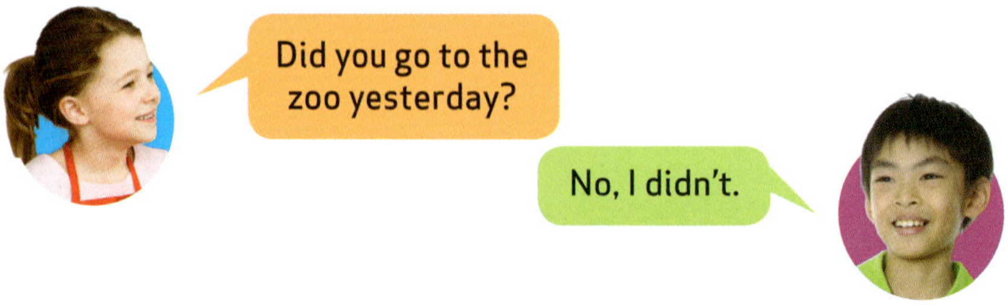
Did you go to the zoo yesterday?
No, I didn't.

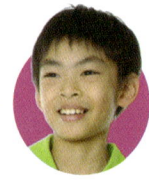

10 **Match the verbs. Test your partner. Then make sentences.**

1 go	**a** ate
2 have	**b** saw
3 get	**c** had
4 eat	**d** went
5 is	**e** got
6 see	**f** was

go

went

We went to the theatre yesterday.

11 **Use the verbs from 10 in the past. Then say.**

1 Yesterday, I ❓ two bananas before school.

2 Susie ❓ you a present from the gift shop.

3 At the weekend, I ❓ a play at the theatre.

4 The school trip ❓ great.

5 We ❓ a lot of fun on our trip to the zoo.

6 They ❓ to a national park on Friday.

12 **Ask and answer. Use the words from the boxes.**

last weekend   last year   yesterday

eat   get   go   have   is   learn   like   see   visit   walk

Where did you go yesterday?

I went to the art gallery. It was fun.

13 **Look at the paintings. Do you like them? Which is your favourite? Compare with a partner.**

177

14 **Listen and read. Then match paragraphs 1–4 to pictures a–d.**

> **CONTENT WORDS**
>
> artist   colourful   funny   happy   impressionist   oil painting
> painter   sad   sketch   strange   watercolour

a

The Little Giants by Francisco de Goya

b

Spring 1573 by Giuseppe Arcimboldo

c

Old Man with his Head in his Hands by Vincent Van Gogh

d

Haystacks at Giverny by Claude Monet

At the Art Gallery

1 *@Amylovesart* Last week, I went to the National Gallery with my mum. Was it boring? No way! Did you know there are lots of messages in paintings and there are lots of different styles? This was my favourite painting. An Italian artist painted it in the 16ᵗʰ century. It looks like a face, doesn't it? It is but it's also lots of other things. Every bit of the face and body is a different spring fruit, vegetable or flower. I like this picture because it's pretty, colourful and clever. It shows humans and nature.

What are your favourite paintings? Please write and tell me.

2 *@ConchiConchi* I love this painting from the Prado Museum in Madrid. There are children in it. They're playing a funny game. The young children look happy but the older children look a bit tired. Mum says the artist painted it in the 19ᵗʰ century just before he stopped hearing. He went deaf. That's really sad. I think the painter became an artist for the king of Spain.

3 *@MattieMonstreParis* My grandmother has this painting in her living room. It isn't the original; someone copied it. A French impressionist painter painted the original and it's in the Musée d'Orsay in Paris. Anyway this reminds me of summer. It's on a farm probably. My grandmother says this is one of the painter's best paintings. He painted another twenty paintings like this with different colours. That's a bit strange, isn't it?

4 *@MoniqueNetherlands* This is in a museum near my house in the Netherlands. It's by a Dutch painter. It isn't an oil painting, it's just a pencil sketch with watercolour. This painting is sad but I think it's interesting. I mean, what's that man thinking? Why is he so sad? Maybe it's a bit scary, too because perhaps something horrible happened. The painter painted this in 1882. My dad says the painter was very ill. He was in hospital with a mental illness.

@Amylovesart Wow! So many great paintings in museums all over the world. I'd like to see them one day!

15 💬 **Look at 14. Answer the questions in your notebook.**

1. Which painter painted for the king?
2. Which painter had an illness?
3. Which painter painted fruit and vegetable people?
4. Which painter painted a painting twenty times?

16 💬 **Student A: Close your book. Answer your partner's questions about Guiseppe Arcimbaldo and Vincent Van Gogh. What can you remember?**

Student B: Close you book. Answer your partner's questions about Claude Monet and Francisco de Goya. What can you remember?

1. Where did he come from?
2. What did he paint?
3. When did he paint it?
4. What's interesting about the painting?
5. Do you like it?

Where did Vincent Van Gogh come from?

He came from the Netherlands.

Yes, that's right.

 **THINK BIG** **What do you like to see most in paintings; people, animals or nature? Why?**

PROJECT

17 💬 **Find out about another famous painting. Then present it to the class.**

I went to the National Gallery of Art in Washington, D.C. It's a famous art gallery. I saw a famous painting by Pierre-Auguste Renoir. It's called *A Girl with a Watering Can*. It was painted in 1876. I think it's a beautiful painting.

179

18 Look, listen and read. Did Mary see the play?

Bill: I didn't see you outside the theatre last night. Where were you?

Mary: We were late. First, the car didn't start. Then we didn't catch the bus because we didn't get to the bus stop on time. We didn't arrive before the play started so we didn't see any of the actors go into the theatre.

Bill: But you saw the play.

Mary: No, we didn't. Dad didn't have the tickets. They were in the pocket of his other jacket!

I/You/He/She/It/We/They	**didn't** play.
	didn't walk.
	didn't stay.
I/You/He/She/It/We/They	**didn't** go.
	didn't see.
	didn't come.

19 Write sentences in your notebook.

1 The bus/not stop/at our bus stop.

2 The play/not start/at 5 o' clock.

3 Erol/not see/any actors.

4 George/not take/photos.

5 They/not visit/the national park.

6 Dina and Eva/not like/the art gallery.

20 **The sentences are false. Correct them in your notebook.**

1 Last summer, Tom went to Spain.
Tom **?** to Spain. He **?** to France.

2 Yesterday, May played tennis with Carmen.
May **?** tennis with Carmen. She **?** tennis with Jenny.

3 Last week, Sam visited the London Aquarium.
Sam **?** the London Aquarium. He **?** the Tower of London.

4 Last month, we learned about rocks at school.
We **?** about rocks at school. We **?** about plants.

5 Three days ago, Eduardo saw a play.
Eduardo **?** a play. He **?** a film at the cinema.

6 Hundreds of years ago people watched TV.
People **?** TV. They **?** shows or plays.

21 **Read Amanda's list of holiday activities. In your notebook, write about the things she did and didn't do.**

go to Ellis Island ✓
see the Statue of Liberty ✓
visit the Guggenheim museum ✓
travel to Yosemite national park ✗   eat dinner with Aunt Harriet ✗
get tickets for a Broadway show ✗   write postcards to friends ✗
go shopping ✓

22 **Now close your books and try to remember. What did Amanda do? What didn't Amanda do? Use the words from the box for help.**

aquarium   art gallery   concert hall   go shopping
meet Aunt Harriet   museum   national park   theatre   zoo

23 **Tell your partner about five things you did on holiday last year and five things you didn't do.**

I went to the aquarium but I didn't go to the museum.

I went to a farm. I saw lots of animals. I didn't go to the aquarium.

The World Stage

1   Today, people everywhere enjoy watching films and television. But TV and cinema are quite new. Before films and television, people didn't have lots of entertainment. Instead they did things at home or they sometimes went to theatres to see plays or performances. Watching performances on stage didn't stop being popular. Today around the world, different countries have different types of stage performances that were popular in the past and are popular today.

2   There were theatres in Greece more than 2,000 years ago. Most Greek cities had a theatre. Greek plays were funny or sad but all of them taught important lessons about life. In those times, all the actors were men or boys and there was a chorus with people singing. Greek plays are still popular today and every summer people enjoy watching them in open-air theatres.

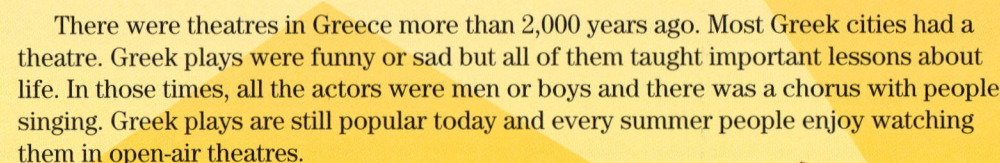

24 **Work with a partner and guess. When did these things happen? Match the sections to make sentences.**

1	The first cinema opened	the Moondog Coronation Ball in Cleveland, Ohio,	in 1765. They called it an animal menagerie.
2	The first zoo opened	in Vienna, Austria,	in 1952.
3	Families bought their first TVs in	in New Orleans,	in 1896. All the films were silent.
4	The first rock concert was	in the U.S.,	in 1945. They cost €100.

180
25 **Listen and read. Where did the first theatre open?**

> **CONTENT WORDS**
> dramatic   entertainment   flamenco   open-air theatre
> performance   play   popular   puppet   show   stage

26 **Find these numbers in 25. Complete the sentences.**

1   2,000 years ago, there ❓ .

2   In the 1600s, people ❓ .

3   Hundreds of years ago, flamenco ❓ .

4   In the 11ᵗʰ century, people from ❓ .

3   William Shakespeare made theatre popular in England about 400 years ago. Shakespeare wrote many plays. People laughed and cried when they watched them in the 1600s and they still do today. Today you can see his plays in theatres all over the world in many different languages and everybody loves them. One of his most famous plays is *Romeo and Juliet*.

4   Music and dance are also popular stage shows. In Spain, people love watching performances of flamenco dancing and music. Flamenco comes from Southern Spain. It started hundreds of years ago when people moved to Spain from the East. Usually there's a guitar and men and women dance. 'Palmeros' clap in a special way with the dancers. Flamenco music and dance are very dramatic. Together, the music and dance tell a story.

5   In Vietnam, people enjoy watching an interesting kind of theatre called Mua Roi Nuoc. There aren't any actors – only puppets. The puppets are on a stage filled with water. People from the Red River Delta began doing Mua Roi Nuoc puppet shows in the 11th century but people still watch performances today. They're magical.

6   TV and cinema are great fun but stage performances made us happy through history and they continue to make us smile or cry.

27   **Read and choose the correct answer.**

1   Greek plays were   **a** always sad.   **b** all about life.
2   Shakespeare was   **a** an actor.   **b** very popular.
3   Flamenco is a performance of   **a** music and dance.   **b** a long story.
4   The Mua Roi Nuoc puppets   **a** are very big.   **b** are on water.

28   **Work with a partner. Ask and answer.**

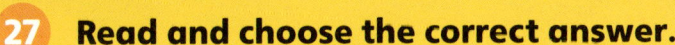

going to concerts   going to the cinema   going to the theatre
playing cards   playing musical instruments
playing video games   singing with your family   watching TV

1   Which of the things in the box do you do in your free time?
2   What did people do in your country in the past in their free time?

THINK BIG   **Which do you prefer watching; dance, theatre or film? Why?**

182

29 **Read and find. Then listen and check.**

> Sentences have got subjects, verbs and objects. They appear in this order:
> We had fun.
> They didn't see a show.
> Did you see a sea lion show?

1 Did you visit a zoo?

2 Yes, I did.

3 I saw elephants and zebras.

30 **Find the subjects, verbs and objects.**

1 Did she visit a dairy farm?

2 They didn't see any scary paintings.

3 I learned about rocks.

4 Did you see a film?

31 **Put the words in order to make detail sentences.**

1 went | We | to the National Gallery.

2 old and new paintings. | saw | I

3 love | I | painting and listening to guides.

4 Our class | famous artists. | learned about

32 **Find the title, topic sentence and final sentence. Now write the paragraph in your notebook.**

> It was lots of fun.   My favourite school trip
> We usually go on school trips every summer.

183

33 Listen, read and repeat.

1 **nt**   2 **ld**   3 **nd**   4 **st**

184

34 Listen and find. Then say.

tent   **chi**ld   **ha**nd   **ne**st

185

35 Listen and blend the sounds.

1	p-l-a-n-t	plant		

1 p-l-a-n-t plant   2 o-l-d   old
3 c-o-l-d   cold   4 b-a-n-d band
5 s-a-n-d   sand   6 a-n-t   ant
7 ch-e-s-t   chest   8 f-a-s-t fast

186

36 Read aloud. Then listen and chant.

An old, cold band
Playing in the sand.
A fast ant
Playing in a tent.

37 **Complete the chart using the words from the box.**

| basketball dance drawing English football Maths painting Science swimming |

a  **b** **c**

Sports	Arts	School Subjects
?	?	?
?	?	?
?	?	?

38 **Work with a partner. Talk about your talents.**

 Do you like Maths?

No, I don't. But I like Art! I'm good at painting.

PROJECT

39 **Have a Talent Show. Share your talent with the class.**

Class Talent Show

40 **Look and say the places.**

1
2
3
4
French Paintings

41 **Complete the dialogue. Then role play.**

A: Hey! How are you, Claudia?

B: I'm fine, Dad.

A: What did you ¹❓ today?

B: I ²❓ have lessons today. I ³❓ on a school trip with my class.

A: Cool! Where ⁴❓ you ⁵❓ ?

B: We went to the ⁶❓ .

A: That sounds fun. Did you ⁷❓ it?

B: Yes. I ⁸❓ . It ⁹❓ really fun but I ¹⁰❓ see the monkeys. They were hiding!

42 **Work with a partner. Plan your own school trip. Then present it to the class.**

Where did you go?

What did you do?

What did you learn?

Did you like it?

Why/Why not?

> We went to a toy museum. We saw some very old toys. Some of them were a hundred years old! We liked it a lot.

I Can

- talk about actions in the past and places to visit.
- talk about paintings.
- write sentences with a subject, verb and object.

How Well Do I Know It? Can I Use It?

1 **Think about it. Read and draw. Practise.**

😄 I know this.   😐 I need more practice.   😟 I don't know this.

		PAGES			
1	**Food:** bread, mustard, onions, turkey…	112	😄	😐	😟
2	**Healthy habits:** ate breakfast, drank water, got enough sleep, rode my bike…	128	😄	😐	😟
3	**School trip places:** aquarium, museum, national park, theatre…	144	😄	😐	😟
4	**School trip activities:** saw a penguin show, saw a film, learned about rocks, saw a play…	145	😄	😐	😟
5	**Is** there **any** pizza? Yes, there is. There**'s some** pizza.	116–117	😄	😐	😟
6	**How much** food is there? There's **an** onion, **a lot of** meat, **a little** ketchup and **many** potatoes.	120–121	😄	😐	😟
7	**Did** you **get** enough exercise? Yes, I **did**. **Did** you **get** enough sleep? No, I **didn't**.	132–133	😄	😐	😟
8	They **changed** clothes and we **tidied** the room. She **exercised** and he **dropped** in.	136–137	😄	😐	😟
9	Where **did** they **go**? They **went** to the zoo.	148–149	😄	😐	😟
10	I **didn't phone** and he **didn't come**.	152–153	😄	😐	😟

188

2 Get ready.

A Complete the dialogue with Kelly's answers. Then listen and check.

Kelly: Hello?

Dad: Hi, Kelly. It's Dad.

Kelly: Oh, hi, Dad!

Dad: How is New York City?

Kelly: ¹ 🔑

Dad: What did you do yesterday?

Kelly: ² 🔑

Dad: That sounds fun. Did you like it?

Kelly: ³ 🔑

Dad: Great. So, when is your football game?

Kelly: ⁴ 🔑

Dad: I see. Did you get enough sleep last night?

Kelly: ⁵ 🔑

Dad: That's good. Did you eat breakfast this morning?

Kelly: ⁶ 🔑

Dad: That sounds delicious! Well, good luck today. Call me after your game.

Kelly: OK, Dad. Talk to you later.

Dad: Bye.

Kelly's answers

a Yes, Dad. I ate a big pancake.

b Yes, it was great! We saw a lot of interesting paintings.

c Yes, I went to bed at 7:00 last night.

d We went to the Museum of Modern Art.

e It's today. It starts at 2:00.

f It's really cool. We arrived yesterday afternoon.

B Practise the dialogue in **A** with a partner. Make up your own answers.

1
2
3
4
5
6
7
8
9

3 **Get set.**

 STEP 1 Cut out the cards on page 161 of your Activity Book.

 STEP 2 Read Dialogue 1 below. Then place the cards in order to create Dialogue 2.

 STEP 3 Look at the pictures below. Choose the picture that illustrates each dialogue. Now you're ready to **Go!**

 4 **Go!**

A With a partner, practise Dialogue 1. Change parts and practise again.

A: Where did you go yesterday?

B: We went to a big art gallery.

A: What did you do there?

B: We looked at some paintings.

A: Did you like it?

B: Not really. The paintings were strange.

A: What did you eat for dinner?

B: I ate a big pizza. It was delicious.

A: Did you get enough sleep last night?

B: No. I went to bed at 11:00.

A: Did you eat breakfast this morning?

B: No. I drank some water. I feel a bit ill.

Where did you go yesterday?

We went to a big art gallery.

B Use your cards to act out Dialogue 2 with a partner.

5 **Write about yourself in your notebook.**

- Where did you go last weekend?
- What did you do there?
- Did you like it?
- What or who did you see?

- Did you get enough sleep last night?
- Did you eat a healthy breakfast?
- Did you get any exercise?

All About Me   Date:

How Well Do I Know It Now?

6 **Think about it. Look at page 160 and your notebook. Draw again.**

A Use a different colour.

B Read and think.

I can ask my teacher for help.

I can practise.

7 **Rate this Checkpoint.**

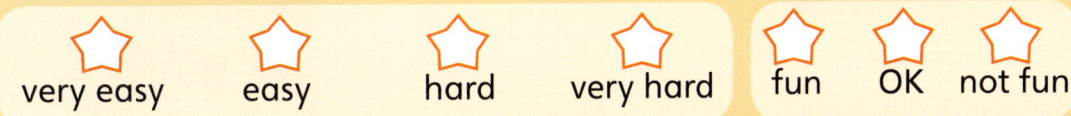

very easy   easy   hard   very hard   fun   OK   not fun

1
2
3
4
5
6
7
8
9

Units 7–9 Exam Preparation

– Part A –

 Look at the pictures. What did Alex do last week?
Listen and draw a line from the day to the correct picture.
There is one example.

Sunday

Monday

Tuesday

Wednesday

Thursday

Friday

Saturday

– Part B –

Look at the pictures and read the story. Write some words to complete the sentences about the story. You can use 1, 2 or 3 words.

Jane lives with her parents and her sister, Lily, near a national park. Janes likes riding her bike in the forest there. Last Sunday, Jane and her family went for a walk after lunch. They saw a woman. She was painting flowers. "That's very nice!" said Jane and the woman smiled.

Examples

Jane's sister is called _____Lily_____.
Jane's house is close to a _national park_.

Questions

1   Last Sunday, Jane had lunch and went for a _____ in the forest.
2   There was a _____ who was painting in the forest.
3   Jane thought the painting of the flowers was _____.

Jane talked to her uncle the next day. "Do you want to come to the art gallery with me, Jane?" he asked. They went to the art gallery that afternoon. The woman from the forest was there, too! "Welcome to my art gallery!" she said. Jane saw the painting with the flowers again. She really liked it so the woman gave it to her. Now the painting is in Jane's bedroom.

4   Jane's uncle invited her to _____.
5   The woman gave Jane a _____.
6   Jane put the painting in her _____.

Wordlist

Find these words in your language. Then write in your notebook.

Unit 1	Page
do my homework	4
eat breakfast	4
get dressed	4
go home	4
go to school	4
go to the park	4
play football	4
play video games	4
wake up	4
watch TV	4
seven thirty	5
time	5
brush your teeth	6
face	6
morning	6
like	7
put on his shoes	7
afternoon	8
evening	8
seven fifty	8
eat dinner	9
ride my bike	9
bacteria	10
cough	10
decay	10
germ	10
gum disease	10
have a shower	10
health	10
healthy	10
ill	10
skin	10
sneeze	10
sweat	10
wash your hands	10
dark	14

	Page
different	14
globe	14
half-turn	14
map	14
time zone	14
chat	15
e-pals	15
online	15
subject	16
verb	16
bone	17
cake	17
note	17
shape	17

Unit 2	Page
cashier	20
farmer	20
firefighter	20
nurse	20
police officer	20
scientist	20
student	20
waiter	20
farm	21
fire station	21
hospital	21
laboratory	21
police station	21
shop	21
university	21
school	24
create	26
drawing	26
fashion designer	26
gallery	26
material	26

	Page
painting	26
pattern	26
photographer	26
photo shoot	26
piece of art	26
professional	26
sculpture	26
sketch	26
unusual	26
donate	30
be proud of	31
collect	31
community	31
contest	31
get lost	31
rubbish	31
Spain	31
skates	33
ski	33
skin	33
smile	33
smoke	33
space	33
spoon	33
star	33
stop	33
storm	33

Unit 3	Page
clean my room	36
do the dishes	36
feed the fish	36
make my bed	36
practise the piano	36
study for a test	36
take out the rubbish	36
walk the dog	36

always	37	boy	49	stonefish	64
chores	37	joy	49	surroundings	64
day	37	May	49	tree bark	64
twins	37	pay	49	tree frog	64
sometimes	37	ray	49	canary	68
say	38	soy	49	goldfish	68
alarm clock	39	toy	49	million	68
never	39			parakeet	68
usually	41	**Unit 4**	**Page**	rodent	68
adult	42	animal	58	alligator	69
amount	42	bear	58	gecko	69
cash	42	camel	58	hamster	69
cents	42	deer	58	snake	69
clean	42	lizard	58	tarantula	69
cost	42	owl	58	topic sentence	70
earn	42	penguin	58	bean	71
euro	42	sea lion	58	boil	71
let (someone) know	42	shark	58	coin	71
pocket money	42	toucan	58	foe	71
save	42	desert	59	meat	71
stranger	42	forest	59	oil	71
subtotal	42	ice and snow	59	peach	71
tidy	42	jungle	59	tea	71
times a week	42	lake	59	toe	71
total	42	mountain	59		
wash	42	ocean	59	**Unit 5**	**Page**
business	46	rainforest	59	cloudy	74
entrance	46	trick	60	cold	74
pavement	46	well	60	cool	74
share	46	blend in	64	hot	74
shovel	46	bottom of the sea	64	rainy	74
task	46	camouflage	64	snowy	74
goat	47	chameleon	64	sunny	74
noodles	47	eat	64	today	74
tiring	47	polar bear	64	warm	74
capital letters	48	rock	64	windy	74
title	48	stone	64	coat	75

Wordlist

jumper	75	flowers	90	glass	103
raincoat	75	horrible	90	glow	103
sandals	75	look	90	plant	103
scarf	75	lovely	90	play	103
shorts	75	nice	90	plum	103
sunglasses	75	pie	90		
hike	76	smell	90	**Unit 7**	**Page**
snack	76	soft	90	bread	112
yesterday	76	sound	90	cucumbers	112
average	80	soup	90	from	112
climate	80	sweet	90	green	112
degrees Celsius	80	taste	90	lettuce	112
dry	80	terrible	90	mushrooms	112
extreme	80	tight	90	olives	112
mild	80	danger	93	onions	112
minus	80	avoid	96	peppers	112
temperature	80	brain	96	tomato sauce	112
tourist	80	echo	96	turkey	112
sleep	81	fresh	96	fridge	114
cricket	84	information	96	surprise	114
kite	84	senses	96	blood	118
fill up	85	sound waves	96	bone	118
sledging	85	taste buds	96	brain	118
snow fight	85	tongue	96	energy	118
detail sentences	86	smelly	100	fat/water soluble	118
swim	87	clean	101	iron	118
scar	87	look after	101	muscle	118
scout	87	stink	101	teeth	118
slim	87	wet	101	vitamin	118
slow	87	final sentence	102	blueberries	122
snail	87	black	103	boiled/fried eggs	122
swan	87	block	103	cereal	122
sweet	87	blow	103	honey	122
		flag	103	oats	122
Unit 6	**Page**	flip-flops	103	porridge	122
delicious	90	fly	103	toast	122
feel	90	glad	103	doughnut	123